STRANGERS HAVE THE BEST CANDY

Margaret Meps Schulte

With original illustrations by the author

How talking to strangers leads to a life
of crazy adventure and lasting friendship

Strangers Have the Best Candy

Disclaimer: The events described in this book are true as I remember them. Some names and details have been changed to protect the privacy of those poor, unsuspecting souls who had no idea they were talking to someone who was going to publish a book about them.

The purpose of this memoir is to entertain. The author and Choose ART shall have neither liability nor responsibility to any person or entity with respect to any loss or damage caused, or alleged to have been caused, directly or indirectly, by the information contained in this book.

If you do not wish to be bound by the above, you may return this book to the publisher for a full refund.

10 9 8 7 6 5 4 3 2

Published in the United States of America

CHOOSE
ART

1meps.com/chooseartbooks

ISBN 978-0-9916076-0-0

Cover design, illustrations, and photography by Margaret Meps Schulte
Interior design and illustrations by Margaret Meps Schulte

For
Dad and Barry,
who are not only featured in these pages,
but whose loving encouragement made them possible.

GRATITUDE

To three funny guys who were eager to read
this book, but who didn't live long enough:

"Life is much easier if one doesn't have to make sense all the time."

Bill Brown

"Curious George wants to know, what the heck are 'naughty bits?'"

Stevie Schulte

"By snail mail, cat mail, carrier pigeon, dragon mail, owl mail, string and tin can
voice, grapevine, trained toad mail, loud voice (can't you hear me calling you?),
telephone, satellite phone, cell phone, trained butterfly mail, mystic psychic
mail, letter, cereal box, or even the possibility of in-person."

Philip Wilson

To Patricia McNeely, for reminding me I wasn't crazy (even though I am).

To Nora Allen, the Bacon-Kischner family, Linda Knepper, Jacqui MacConnell,
Leilani McCoy & Bob Purnell, the Miller family, and Sharon & David
Stellrecht, who gave this nomadic sailor a warm, cozy place to write.

To my silent companions in the libraries of North Carolina, Georgia,
Florida, Ohio, and Washington. How could I not write a book
when surrounded by thousands of them every day?

Especially, to all the people whose stories are in this book.
It's not my book. It's yours.

CONTENTS

Strangers Have the Best *What?*..1

Candy Everywhere I Go...9

Little Miss Sunshine 19

I Wrote a Story About You in My Head 27

Facing Danger (Because I Had No Other Choice) 35

What's the Worst Thing That Can Happen?..........................45

Better Than Google 51

When Receiving Is a Gift..65

Always Say Yes… 69

…And Always Take All Your Stuff 75

Writing My Plans in the Sand...89

The Best Way to Talk Is Not to 99

Taming Chipmunks...109

Real People Are Not a Tourist Attraction 133

I Met This Crazy Lady Once (and She Was Me) 139

Tagging Along With Experts...147

In or Out? The Dilemma in Every Parade 159

Stay a While With Me 171

Introductions Are Priceless..179

Getting Out of the Car..187

A Couple of Scavenger Hunts (Including My Biggest Flop) ...193

Meps' Theory of Travel Relativity..203

I Should Have Bought a Lottery Ticket 215

Homebodies 227

Kindred Spirits 239

"Always do what you are afraid to do."
Ralph Waldo Emerson

CHAPTER 1

STRANGERS HAVE THE BEST *WHAT?*

The sun set over blue tropical waters as I swung gently in a hammock at Bahia Honda, a state park in the Florida Keys. It was a Thursday evening in May, a few days after my 29th birthday. The hammock was new; it had been a birthday gift.

"Barry?" I said.

"Hmm?" My husband was swinging in his own hammock, a few feet away.

All our friends have to go to work tomorrow. Isn't that weird?

"All our friends have to go to work tomorrow. Isn't that weird?"

He was unmoved by my epiphany. "I guess so."

Listening to the distant thunder of waves crashing on the beach, I envisioned our friend Andy, at home in his apartment. Back in northern Virginia, he'd be packing his lunch, folding his laundry, cooking dinner, maybe reading a book or watching TV. In the morning, he would take the bus to a government office and sit at his desk, talk on the phone, review documents. He'd take a lunch break, do more of the same work in the afternoon, and go home at the end of the day. The next day would bring the same familiar routine.

A month earlier, my life had been similar. Then we quit our jobs, gave up our apartment, and stored our belongings. We packed our Honda Civic with camping equipment and started driving south, staying at inexpensive state parks and free national forest campgrounds. We thought we had enough savings to travel like this through the summer. In the fall, we'd settle down again, find jobs, and resume a life with furniture and responsibilities. Maybe in Milwaukee.

For the first couple of weeks, it felt like a normal vacation. But on that evening in May, I recognized that I had left my old life behind, and I didn't know if I would ever return. The absolute freedom was exhilarating and terrifying at the same time.

I didn't know that this pursuit of freedom would define my life for decades, not months.

That night in the hammock, something inside me was set free. The world became a different place. I became a rule-breaker, a risk-taker, challenging the rules that I'd naively accepted as requirements for a good life.

The first rule I broke was the one about having a well-paying, stable job, one my parents would be proud of. I'd left a lucrative freelance business, turned my back on a Department of Defense security clearance. I was glad to be free of that heavy responsibility, but worried about how long our savings would last.

I needn't have worried. Living in campgrounds was so cheap, we couldn't spend money as fast as our mutual funds were accruing it.

The day after my epiphany in the hammock, Barry and I drove to the end of the road, to Key West. It was on a streetcorner there that we met James and had a series of encounters that forced me revisit some really big rules: *Don't talk to strangers. Don't get into a stranger's car. Don't go into a stranger's house. Don't take candy from strangers.*

Those rules are written for children. To a small, vulnerable child, strangers are dangerous people with the power to harm. Without the judgment to know whether a particular stranger is safe or not, children have to avoid all of them.

I'm not a child any more. I'm not even a parent or a grandparent who needs to set a good example.

Why should I follow these rules as an adult? Why limit myself?

In the years since my epiphany, I haven't found strangers to be intrinsically more dangerous than non-strangers. Along the way, I've found that strangers have the best candy.

I never know what I'll receive from a stranger. Sometimes, it's just a brief, friendly conversation that cheers me up when I'm lonely. Sometimes, it's a piece of information that I wouldn't have learned otherwise. My willingness to talk with anyone has brought me once-in-a-lifetime experiences, flashes of insight, unexpected gifts, delicious meals, and gracious hospitality.

I once heard a story — from a stranger, of course — about how giving candy to strangers actually saved his life.

He was the owner of a Mom 'n' Pop grocery store in tiny Summit, South Dakota. Of the town's 267 residents, he and his family were the only African-Americans. They had moved there after he got out of the Army, because he and his wife wanted to raise their family in a safe place, a small town far from the big city.

It was while he was stationed in Iraq that his life was saved by candy. He and a group of soldiers routinely patroled Baghdad in an armored vehicle. Each day, when they departed their compound, they would see the same little boys playing in the streets along their route. The soldiers would often toss goodies to the boys in the street.

One day, they went on patrol via their usual route, waving and tossing candy and bottled water to the kids as they went by. When they came back, though, the boys were very agitated. Although they didn't share a common language, they stopped the vehicle, waving their arms and pointing at the road ahead. "They didn't want us to go that way, so we stopped and checked it out," he told me.

They found that someone had come along in the few hours they were gone and planted a row of powerful bombs in the road, linked in a daisy chain. In their hurry to dig up the ground and install the bombs, they paid no attention to the children who watched them. It was those same children who made sure their friends with the candy didn't set off the deadly daisy-chain bomb.

"Those kids saved all our lives," said the grocer, with a shake of his head. "I wouldn't be here today."

When I meet someone who is from a very different background, the things they share with me open a window into a whole world I've never dreamed of. We may make a deep connection and move right past the superficial into subjects that are very dear to our hearts.

In one memorable conversation, in a tiny town in Montana, a stranger gave me both insight into a different world *and* an incredibly valuable, one-of-a-kind gift.

Barry and I were in Hot Springs, a miniscule town (pop. 550) on the Flathead Indian Reservation, 51 miles from the nearest interstate.

My dearly departed friend, Bill Brown, told me that the modern-day definition of "The Frontier" was any place further than two hours from the interstate. I think he would have made an exception for Hot Springs, Montana. It was only one hour from I-90, but was definitely at the edge of the known world. It was actually bigger than St. Regis, which was right at the interstate, but wasn't actually a town. St. Regis was only a Census-Designated Place, a fancy way of saying 350 people who lived next to a freeway on-ramp.

I had heard about Hot Springs from a friend in Seattle, who told me the conversations that went on in the hot pools, between locals and travelers, were not to be missed.

She was right.

Neck-deep in warm, relaxing water, Barry and I started talking
with two men who were staying at the historic Symes hotel.
Perhaps it was the surroundings, or the sulfurous water, but the conversation quickly turned very deep and serious. We talked frankly
about religion, spirituality, and existentialism. Both of the men, who
were strangers to each other, were Christians, but with very different
beliefs, so it was a lively conversation. They were taken aback and
intrigued when I said, without rancor, "I'm not a Christian, but I
appreciate and respect people who are."

A while later, after we'd been talking for over an hour, one of the
men told me he had a book he wanted to give me. "It's very old," he
said, "and if I give it to you, you have to promise me that you'll read
it."

He was a Native American businessman who was supervising a
nearby highway construction project. In his current life, he was very
successful, even wealthy, but he'd grown up on a reservation amongst
poverty and squalor. Intrigued by his offer, I promised to read whatever he gave me.

Because of his early work schedule, he said farewell and left before
the rest of us did. He didn't mention the book again, and I presumed
that he'd changed his mind or forgotten.

A few hours later, when Barry and I came back from dinner, I
was surprised to find a large, heavy parcel sitting on the windshield of
our van, which was parked in the hotel parking lot. Whatever it was,
it was wrapped in many plastic grocery bags, so I carried it into our
room before unwrapping it.

I never saw the man again.

Inside, I found an antique family Bible, with yellowed pages and a worn binding. Turning to the title page, I gave a little gasp.

The book was certainly old, as he had said. Printed in 1859, the unexpected gift I held in my hands was over 150 years old.

I never saw the man again to thank him.

Magical wishy-wash

The Bible was a priceless gift. Yet it wasn't the most valuable gift I've received from a stranger.

Once I have met a person, they are, by definition, never again a stranger. There's a little miracle, a point in time when a person goes from "stranger" to "not-stranger." The famous poet, William Butler Yeats, once said, "There are no strangers. Only friends I have not met yet."

Over and over, I've met people in the most unlikely circumstances who have gone all the way from stranger, to not-stranger, to friend. Because of this, I never know when the gift of friendship is, literally, just around the corner.

I once received the gift of friendship in a coin-operated laundromat known as The Soap Bubble. Kris, who I met there, simply calls it a laundry. My Dad would call it a wishy-wash. I call it magic.

I've been finding this magic since I had my epiphany in the hammock. Talking to strangers, getting to know them, and accepting the gift that is their story and their friendship. To me, it has become as easy as falling off a log.

But I know it's not that easy for others. That's why I'm sharing these stories.

Here are the laughing, crying, topless, boozing, entertaining, and enlightening strangers I have found in the world. Here are the ones who sail in little boats, who fly on big airplanes, who ride their bicycles thousands of miles. Here are the ones who stay home. Here are the mundane, the quirky, the disturbing, and the downright amazing people of this world. Here are their stories, their insights, and their gifts.

Here is the candy that strangers have shared with me. It's the best.

CHAPTER 2

CANDY EVERYWHERE I GO

I was sitting with my friends, Mike and Donna, in Jennie's Diner on US Route 30 in Pennsylvania. Jennie's is an iconic old-fashioned roadside diner, the prefab 1950's kind with a shiny stainless-steel exterior and lots of formica inside. The waitresses were super-efficient, fast-moving women who didn't need a pad and pencil to keep track of complicated, multi-part orders.

"Wait 'til you see the portions!" Mike crowed.

Our conversation started with food, but soon turned to travel and what there was to see in this part of eastern Pennsylvania. Just up the road was a train museum, and they told me about a life-sized replica of Thomas the Tank Engine that was really cool. "It's almost always out on tour, though," Donna warned me. "You can't count on seeing it if you go that way."

Our food arrived, and we dove into fluffy pancakes the size of Manhattan.

"Traveling is easy for you," said Donna, "you have friends everywhere you go." I tried to explain that I didn't already have friends everywhere, I just made new friends as I went along. But she insisted that her life, which centered on working and taking care of her mother in rural Pennsylvania, didn't allow her to meet and talk with new people.

At the end of our meal, all of us were a little sad. It was time to say goodbye after a three-day visit, and we didn't have concrete plans to get together in the near future. We stepped out into the parking lot

"Would you look at that!"

of the diner, and they turned to me in shock. "Would you look at that!"

Right in front of us, on a flatbed trailer, was the full-sized, brightly-colored Thomas the Tank Engine. We walked over for a closer look, arriving at the same time as a couple of curious truck drivers. I struck up a conversation with them, talking about how much fun it would be to drive this truck, instead of the more conventional loads they were waiting for.

One of the drivers had a real twinkle in his eye. He introduced himself as Fred Sanford. "You know, like the TV character!" I smiled; I could see a slight physical resemblance to the 70's sitcom character, a wisecracking black man who ran a junkyard.

I introduced myself, and I shook Fred's hand. Then I turned to Donna and Mike, and as though I'd known Fred for more than five seconds, I introduced them. The group continued chatting for a while, and Fred's comments kept us laughing the entire time. He was a comedian, just like the character from TV.

The other driver was traveling with a small dog. He was also friendly, but a lot more serious. His comments gave us a glimpse of a more lonely life, that of a long-haul trucker on the road, whose solitude was only alleviated by the company of his pet.

Eventually, Thomas' driver came back with his takeout food and pulled away, and the conversation broke up. The two drivers and the little dog walked back to their rigs in the back of the gravel parking lot, under the trees, and Mike and Donna and I walked to our cars.

"I've never done anything like that before!" said Donna, shaking her head.

"Like what?" I asked.

"Like talking with a truck driver I've never met," she admitted.

"See? It's easier than you think," I pointed out.

She remained skeptical, insisting that I was responsible for the serendipity. I had started the conversation with the truck drivers. I had somehow made Thomas the Tank Engine and Fred Sanborn magically appear.

Donna's insistence made me stop and think. Had I done something so special that others couldn't do it? No matter how I looked at it, I couldn't see it that way. I had simply smiled at a couple of truck drivers, discovered they were friendly, and struck up a conversation. When the time was right, we introduced ourselves and shook hands.

The fact that the conversation was entertaining and memorable was luck. But the more conversations I strike up with strangers, the better my odds of finding someone who *is* entertaining and memorable.

The part I can never quite comprehend is that people find *me* entertaining and memorable. For months after he met us at Burning Man, an event in the Nevada desert, Mike had been telling Donna about me and my husband.

"Meps and Barry, Meps and Barry, that's how all his sentences started. He just kept talking about you guys *all* the time," she said. "I was like, 'What is it about these people that's so special?' Then I met you, and all my friends had to listen to me starting my sentences with 'Meps and Barry, Meps and Barry!'"

Mike had been a complete stranger to me only a year earlier, when he showed up at Burning Man in a rented RV. He didn't know a single person there, and the fact that he'd saved his money for several years in order to travel clear across the USA to attend the event, held in one of the most inhospitable environments imaginable, impressed the hell out of me.

One of the founders of Burning Man wrote a list of ten principles that describe the event's culture. Right there, on the first line, under "Radical Inclusion," is this statement: "We welcome and respect the stranger."

When Mike climbed down from the cab of his RV, I didn't just welcome him. I *adopted* him. I introduced myself and my husband and showed Mike how we greet people at Burning Man, with great big hugs instead of wimpy handshakes. I welcomed him to hang out with us, share our food and drink, borrow our costumes, and ask for advice and support. In short, I made him part of my tribe.

Burning Man is difficult to describe, like the blind man and the elephant. To call it a huge art festival, with 60,000 participants, would barely scratch the surface of explanation. It's a temporary city, created in the middle of a harsh desert in the summer, where every single item must be brought in. Yet we leave no trace, removing everything we bring, down to the last tiny sequin. The difference between the one-week event and the other 51 weeks of the year — what we Burners call "the default world" — is the culture. Instead of a commercial event, where people bring their wares to sell, we practice "gifting," where we give unconditionally, without expecting anything in exchange. The tribe is the entire city, and I find myself giving gifts and receiving them from people under remarkable circumstances.

Although I've been interacting with strangers and collecting stories about them for decades, Burning Man has changed the way I think about it.

A couple of years ago, after I left Burning Man, I went into a grocery store with a group of friends. I bought a couple of items, but my friends were still shopping. I was waiting in the front of the store, where all the shopping carts were stored, and there was a dispenser with disinfectant wipes. So I started wiping off the cart-handles and then offering carts to people as they walked into the store.

After a week at Burning Man, it seemed like the most natural thing in the world to do, this little act of service as I waited for my friends. Most of the people thanked me gratefully. But some were freaked out and suspicious. They refused the carts I offered them, taking one of the ones I hadn't wiped off.

That's because they were not used to gifting; they were only used to exchanges. In the non-Burning Man world, when someone does something for us, or hands us something, they always expect us to remunerate them for it. The people who refused carts were probably afraid of what I would ask of them in return.

It's that same fear that prevents many of us from accepting candy from strangers.

My late artistic partner, Philip "MacGyver" Wilson, inspired the title of this book. We went out walking at Burning Man one day, and he was wearing a bright orange t-shirt that he'd had made with block letters that said, "Strangers Have the Best Candy." Over and over, people who saw his shirt would laugh out loud.

The following year at Burning Man, he wore the shirt again, but this time, he carried a bag of candy to hand out to strangers. He was a giant of man, bearded and broad-shouldered, about six and a half feet tall. In addition to the t-shirt with the suspicious message, he was wearing something like a skirt, one of those denim Utilikilts, with God-knows-what under it.

In the gifting culture of Burning Man, every stranger accepted the candy from him without fear.

Barry said that if we did something like that outside of Burning Man, people would react badly. "They might even call the police on you," he said.

Still, I figure that the more gifting I do, the more the world will get used to it. And in the meantime, I can be satisfied with the more customary exchanges we allow ourselves to have with strangers: Handshakes. Names. Smiles.

I was in Yelm, Washington, with Barry and our friend, Tom, on a rare day when the temperature was over 100 degrees Fahrenheit. Tom suggested that we visit a special swimming hole he knew of, but Barry and I hadn't brought bathing suits. Tom assured us that they wouldn't be necessary; the spot

Every stranger accepted candy from him without fear.

*"He just hovered there, staring at my you-know-whats
and giving me a big grin."*

was on private property, and after all, it was Tuesday. He'd been skinny-dipping there many times, he told us.

We drove through cow pastures, parked, and waded a little ways,
clothed, into the Nisqually River. The banks were lined with evergreen trees, and the water rushed over rocks and little rapids and
our ankles. It was totally cool and refreshing, and I started to think
about disrobing — but what was this? Around the corner came an
overloaded rubber raft, packed with a large, boisterous family. Mom,
Dad, and the kids were followed by a flock of additional family members in inner tubes. Then a couple of guys popped out of the woods
directly across the river from us with fishing poles. Another raft, with
a cooler, floated by with two guys in it, whooping and hollering.

I had resigned myself to swimming with my clothes on, when
another person appeared, this time from behind us. A woman strolled

right onto our little private beach. This place was like Grand Central Station!

Shen had a big, friendly smile and was wearing a sarong, holding it up around her breasts with one hand. "Hi! I'm Boopsie," she said. I'm not sure if that was her real name, or if that was a skinny-dipping alias. If so, it was a great skinny-dipping alias.

Boopsie charged into the river and nearly lost her sarong in the current. Tom chivalrously helped her hang onto the errant piece of colorful fabric. At least, I think that's what he was doing. She made her way to a big rock, perched on it like a mermaid, and commenced entertaining us with stories of her prior bathing-suit-free adventures in this spot.

"I was here one time, by myself," she said, "and I couldn't hear anything but the rushing of the water on this rock. Well, along came a helicopter from Fort Lewis, super-low over the water, and I didn't even hear him. Before I realized what was happening, there I was, eye-to-eye with the pilot! He just hovered there, staring at my you-know-whats and giving me a big grin." Barry, Tom, and I grinned at each other, then joined Boopsie out in the river.

Of course, more rafts came by, but when they did, I submerged myself so they wouldn't see my you-know-whats. Boopsie waved at them. Then a helicopter flew by from Fort Lewis, as low as he possibly could, and she waved gleefully at the pilot. I sank down so only my nose was above water, thinking I needed a skinny-dipping alias.

There was more to Boopsie's story, though. Eventually, she took off her sarong and began telling us about her breast cancer, and the series of reconstructive surgeries she was in the middle of. The breasts we could see were only temporary implants designed to stretch the muscles and get her body ready for permanent implants. "These are really hard," she said, poking them to demonstrate, "but the final ones will be soft, like real boobs. Then I'll have nipples tattooed on, too."

My encounter with Boopsie followed a simple pattern. We smiled at each other, made some casual comments, then we introduced ourselves by name. After that, the conversation turned to deeper, more meaningful topics. In a short time, we had gone from funny stories to Boopsie's frank discussion of breast cancer and reconstruction. It was remarkable, not at all the kind of conversation I expected to have with a fellow skinny-dipper.

Sometimes, an encounter is too brief, too fleeting, to exchange names, but we still exchange a friendly, memorable handshake. One of those occurred at a Flying J truck stop near Fancy Gap, in southern Virginia. We had slept in the parking lot in the back of our Ford Club Wagon van, which we call the Squid Wagon. In the morning Barry tumbled out Squidley's back door (it's about 4½ feet down to the ground from our bed) and headed to the bathroom.

A few minutes later, I clambered out that way, too, yawning and finger-combing my tousled hair. Just then, a white SUV with dark tinted windows and Georgia plates parked next to us, and a slender black man got out of the driver's seat. He s-t-r-e-t-c-h-e-d, and as he did, his companion came around the car to take the wheel. She was bright-eyed and round-figured, and she had that characteristic I've-been-riding-too-long limp.

They met on the driver's side, and he surprised her with a big hug. She threw her head back and started laughing; she was still laughing merrily as she slid into the driver's seat and closed the door.

The man stayed beside the car and got out a cigarette. I smiled at him and asked, "What did you say to make her laugh like that?"

He broke into a broad smile himself.

"I haven't been able to drive for 23 years," he said, "you know, problems with my license…I got it all straightened out and got my license two months ago."

"Wow! Congratulations!"

"The last time we did this trip," he continued, "she had to do all the driving." He nodded his head towards the driver's side door. "Now, I think, since I'm the male, that I should be able to do more than I can…but I can't. There are children involved…" That's when I realized, squinting at the tinted windows, that there were two child seats in the car.

He told me they were headed from Atlanta to Pittsburgh, and they'd driven all night. "I have to be responsible; I can't be driving when I'm sleepy." I nodded, and we were silent for a moment, thinking about how dangerous driving can be. I wondered what brought about his 23 lost years, but didn't ask.

"I know what you mean about those long drives," I replied. "Last year, I drove across the country, from Seattle to the Atlantic ocean, by myself. I spent seven weeks."

Now it was his turn to marvel. "Wow, you must have seen a lot," he said. "What did you do?"

"Mostly, I just looked for interesting people to talk with, like yourself!"

We chuckled, wished each other safe travels, and shook hands. His cigarette forgotten, he got into the passenger seat and headed for Pittsburgh with his family.

CHAPTER 3

LITTLE MISS SUNSHINE

If I want candy from strangers, smiling is not optional.

Occasionally, I can spark a conversation with a humorous complaint. However, I absolutely have to be smiling when I do it. If I continue to whine, my conversational partner will find a quick excuse to depart.

I learned this lesson the hard way in the early 90's, when Barry and I tried long-distance bicycle travel.

For over a year, we had been traveling the back roads of the United States in our tiny Honda Civic. We'd lived super-cheaply in campgrounds and national forests, and we'd crisscrossed the country, visiting all our friends and relatives. Still, after we'd been on the road for eight months, we were weary. We stopped in a private campground in Florida and paid for a whole week, but something was missing. It was a small, friendly place, arranged around a small lake, and instead of having private campfire rings at each site, there were several communal campfires each night. Somehow, though, we just couldn't connect with the residents there. They were retired snowbirds in their 60's and 70's, living in giant motorhomes. To them, we probably seemed like a couple of deadbeats, with a subcompact car and a 2-person tent.

Barry and I spent lots of time that week, talking about our nomadic lifestyle and debating what to do next.

I told him that I was feeling lonely. I wanted to talk with more people, and I was afraid that being in the car was isolating us from people.

Nobody would to talk to us, for religious reasons. Oops.

"Let's take a long-distance bicycle trip," I suggested. It was something I'd dreamed of doing since I was a teenager.

It took a few months to get ready, because we had to buy Barry a new bicycle and outfit ourselves with all kinds of fancy gear and high-tech clothing. We didn't bother with many training rides, figuring that we'd just start out slowly, and ride more miles each day.

On my 30th birthday, we started our grand bicycle adventure by riding through Ohio's Amish country. It was scenic, but I was lonelier than ever.

Amish country was a lousy place to start out: The whole point of Amish culture is that of isolation from the modern-day world, which we represented with our high-tech bicycling gear. Basically, we started out riding in a region where nobody would to talk to us, for religious reasons. Oops.

We turned to the north, thinking to ride through Michigan instead.

Then we got word that my mother was in a coma. We put the bicycles aside and rushed to her side. Three weeks and a funeral later, when I returned to my bicycle, I was a changed person. At the young age of 30, I was half an orphan. My Dad was a widower.

Whether I was pedaling the bike, shopping for food, or looking at the scenery, I was always grieving. I cried nonstop, tears running down my face as the cars whizzed by. When we stopped for the night,

I hid in the tent and blew my nose on toilet paper, because our limited weight allowance didn't allow for tissues.

On top of that, we looked really *weird*. The Spandex clothing was effective, but people shied away from us in our unflattering, skin-tight shorts. Besides, we only had three changes of clothing each, so there was always some piece of freshly-laundered intimate apparel flapping on the back of my bike, drying. Our helmets and wrap-around sunglasses made us look like space aliens. Our heavily-loaded touring bicycles intimidated children, often the only other cyclists we saw.

Instead of welcoming us and striking up conversations, people went silent and stared.

I had no patience for them. I got angry and yelled at them when I rode past. "What the hell are you lookin' at?"

The scenery was breathtaking, but I couldn't enjoy it. There were probably all kinds of interesting people along the way, but I couldn't even look them in the eye. It seemed like all I did was pedal, eat macaroni and cheese, and wash my underwear in campground sinks. Standing by the side of the highway, watching Barry deal with yet another broken spoke or flat tire, I imagined what the people in the cars were saying about us:

"Hey, Mom, look at those weirdos!"

"What's *that*?"

"Get off the road, slowpoke!"

After 1,000 miles, I was worn out emotionally, more lonely than ever, and unable to enjoy the world around me. We gave up.

In Madison, Wisconsin, we loaded our bikes on a Greyhound bus and admitted failure.

I have learned quite a bit since that colossal failure. For starters, I have learned to jumpstart my smile.

Sometimes, I'll notice that I am frowning as I walk down the street. I tell myself, "All right, Margaret, that's enough frowning. You are going to smile now." It's a simple matter of moving the muscles in my face, making the corners of my mouth go up. But my face resists it.

"What are you doing? You're grumpy! You're not supposed to be smiling!" say my cheeks.

The thought that my brain and my face are contributing dialogue to two different sides of a conversation is enough to tickle my funny bone. The next thing I know, I'm not only smiling, I have cracked myself up laughing.

You know those times when you can't stop laughing uncontrollably, and you give yourself a jaw cramp? I have a term for that: "Laugh-face."

Sometimes, when my brain and my cheeks get into an argument about smiling, I can give myself laugh-face.

Now, assuming that I haven't overdone it and scared all the strangers away by laughing inappropriately as I walk down the street, I try to catch someone's eye. I'm trying to see if they will look at me and smile back. And not call the funny farm to report a madwoman chuckling her way down the street.

Often, people will studiously try to avoid my eyes. The trick is just to catch one person's eye.

My late brother, Stevie, once told me a great story that illustrated this.

He had his driver's license taken away and was forced to ride the bus to get around town. He was extremely unhappy; a guy with a doctorate who had to ride on smelly city buses with lowlifes. When he got on a bus, he scowled and was grumpy.

One day, he got onto the bus and sat beside the window. A few stops later, a poorly-dressed black man got on and sat down beside him. Stevie stared deliberately out the window, not looking at his seatmate.

That is, until his seatmate turned to him, excitedly, and said, "Hey, bro', how's it goin'?"

Surprised at the familiarity of the man's greeting, he just shrugged without looking at him. The man didn't stop at that. He tapped Stevie on the shoulder and said, in a loud, hurt voice, "Don't you remember me? We was in *jail* together!"

When Stevie related the story to me, he admitted that when his seat mate said that, he finally turned and looked at him.

Stevie remembered the man well. They'd had some good conversations in that jail, the one with the windows overlooking the base-ball park made famous by the movie *Bull Dur-*

Curious Stevie

ham. Although he was completely embarrassed — everybody on the bus now knew his deep, dark secret — he struck up a conversation with his former cellmate, and they had a nice time chatting for the rest of the ride home.

After that, Stevie worked hard to change his attitude. He became very curious about who else was riding the bus, and what neighborhoods the buses were going through. I teased him and called him "Curious George," because he was so intrigued by the world he saw from the window of the bus.

Every day, he and I would talk on the phone about the people he'd met and the places he'd seen. It was a big change from the depressed guy sitting by the bus window, unable to meet the eyes of his fellow passengers.

As Stevie and I both discovered, smiling makes all the difference. Strangers will talk with us, just about anywhere, if we just keep on the sunny side.

I had a chance to practice this over and over when I spent a few hours in the Charlotte, North Carolina airport. I'd taken a redeye flight, overnight from Seattle, and I was bleary-eyed and exhausted, looking forward to my last flight. But when I arrived in Charlotte,

bad weather caused my flight home to be cancelled. Now what?

I took a deep breath and walked to the customer service counter, where a smiling customer is an anomaly. I decided to be that anomaly.

The customer service agent worked out a couple of options for me, and after I made my selection, she printed out my new boarding passes. As she handed them to me, the agent still looked concerned. "I need your luggage tags," she said. I was befuddled by her request, then I realized why she was frowning — she was afraid that my luggage could be misdirected or lost as a result of this change.

"It's OK, I only have carry-on luggage," I said. Her face lit up with a huge smile of relief. "Wow! Lucky! You're good to go, then!"

I had plenty of time to catch my new flight to Orlando. With a sigh of relief, I headed for the nearest bathroom.

It was sparkling clean, and just inside the entrance was a display with free candy, hand lotion, hair products, and feminine supplies. The clue to this largesse was the accompanying tip jar. I had just entered the domain of one of the Charlotte airport's restroom attendants.

This woman, though, was no mere attendant. She was earning her tips as a Bathroom Ambassador.

She bustled around the large bathroom with a cleaning towel, wiping the counters as she greeted women with a cheery hello and a smile. "Hi, how are you today?" She also served as a traffic cop, keeping track of which stalls were in use. "Come on over here, I've got a great room for you, lady!" "Here, take this big one — you've got a lot of luggage."

She made the bathroom so pleasant, I wished they had more comfortable, less-specialized seats in there. I would have stayed for a while. She came over and said hi as I was washing my hands. "If you're going someplace sunny, take me with you!" she quipped.

I don't know," I said, rummaging around for something to put in the tip jar. "You're making it pretty sunny in here!"

Even after my pleasant sojourn in the bathroom, I had over an hour to kill, so I stopped at a Starbucks for a cup of tea. I didn't have to use money for this treat — I paid for it with a gift card my brother had given me for Christmas.

Every time I used that gift card, it made me feel good. It was as if my big brother was giving me a Christmas present over and over.

As I waited, I found myself looking curiously behind me, to see who was next in line. It was a black woman about my age, with a southern accent. She was alone and had no luggage, probably an employee from one of the other shops. We smiled at each other, and then she placed an order very similar to mine. As she fumbled in her purse for the money, I had a brainstorm.

I handed my gift card back to the cashier. "Here, charge hers to my card," I said. The cashier didn't miss a beat, just swiped the card and handed me a new receipt. She probably assumed we knew each other.

The woman in line behind me went through a series of reactions. There was initially confusion as the cashier refused her payment, and then astonishment that a stranger would pay for her order. Apprehension — was I going to ask something of her? And finally, she got it, and was simply grateful. She'd never experienced anything like this before.

"This is one of those pay it forward things, isn't it? Now I have to do something nice for someone else?" she said. I just smiled and said, gently, "Only if you want to." I stepped away to put some milk in my tea, and she followed me across the restaurant.

"Thank you! You really made my day! What's your name?" If I hadn't been carrying a very full cup of tea and two pieces of heavy luggage, I think she would have hugged me.

For many people, the experience of traveling by plane is miserable. The security process takes away all privacy and dignity. When we reassemble our belongings and put our shoes back on, we no longer have autonomy or freedom. Our fate is in someone else's hands.

Our fate, perhaps, but not our experience. Each of us can choose whether to be miserable or not.

On that ill-fated bicycle trip, I chose not to smile. I've grown up a lot since then.

I've learned to smile, to meet people's eyes, to pay it forward. It's part of my diabolical plan to make the world a better place, full of sunshine, flutterbies, and wunny babbits.

Sunshine, flutterbies, and wunny babbits

CHAPTER 4

I WROTE A STORY ABOUT YOU IN MY HEAD

Our brains are wired to judge situations and people; that's a proven scientific fact. Like all human beings, I write a story in my head about each stranger I notice. How do I feel about the story? Attracted? Envious? Repulsed? What about just plain icky?

That's judgment. Without even talking to a stranger, I have judged him or her.

For example, I might see a woman frowning and think, "I bet she's a grouch who never smiles," instead of realizing that she's a normally cheerful woman who just lost her purse.

I might see a man emptying trash cans and think, "I bet he's really boring," instead of finding out that he loves inventing things and spending time with his grandchildren.

Over and over, in my encounters with strangers, I keep relearning this lesson: No person is unworthy of my time. A stranger's true story is always a thousand times more compelling than the one I made up.

So, after I write my story about them, the one in my head, I have to erase it. I have to let it go and let them tell me their real story.

A few days after one of my most challenging, painful ordeals, when I came face-to-face with my own initial judgment, I found a ticket stub in my pocket. I turned it over and read the fine

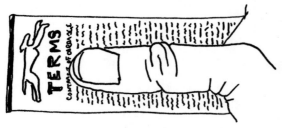

I turned it over and read the fine print.

print, something I had not done when I purchased it: "Seating is first-come, first-served. In case of insufficient seating capacity, passengers will be placed on succeeding schedules that have available seats."

Such a cold, legalistic way to explain the hell I went through in the Greyhound bus terminal in Raleigh, North Carolina.

A friend had dropped me off at the New Bern bus station, a convenience store and gas station situated on the edge of town. It was a dark and moonless night, and the people hanging around the place seemed threatening and scary. There's something odd about where they situate these Greyhound stops — so far out of town that you absolutely have to have a car to reach them, yet the people who need to ride Greyhound buses are the ones who don't have cars.

After an hour of waiting at the awkward gas station, boarding the bus itself was pleasant. It was a new one, clean, with fake leather seats, power outlets for charging electronics, and — Hallelujah! — wi-fi. Fewer than half the seats were occupied, so we each had two seats to ourselves. I thought to myself, "Okay, I can handle 20 hours of this."

About an hour down the road, a man got on at a similar gas station in Goldsboro and took the seat across the aisle from me. He was a slender black man with very short and graying hair, and he was dressed in a curious outfit of all white — white pants, white button-down shirt, white sneakers. His luggage consisted of only a small white trash bag.

I was very curious about my neighbor, but it was late, and the bus was dark, so I didn't strike up a conversation. He pulled a small booklet out of his pocket and read some pages, then put it aside, turned off his reading lamp, and stared out the window.

When the bus arrived in Raleigh, I got off with my carry-on luggage — a heavy backpack and a canvas tote full of snacks and water. I retrieved my enormous purple suitcase from under the bus and went inside to wait about 30 minutes for my next bus.

When I heard an announcement about my bus, I made my way to Door A in a leisurely fashion, about 15 minutes before its departure. There were four people who had formed a line ahead of me.

What happened next was such a surprise that I experienced it with a sort of shocked detachment. This couldn't really be happening to me, could it?

A man came to the door, checked the tickets of the first three people, and let them through. He said something I didn't hear to the fourth person and then turned around.

The man he had spoken to suddenly went berserk, screaming expletives, grabbing the man's shoulder, and threatening him. The gist of his outburst was, "You can't keep me off this $@#%!! bus! I have to muster in at oh-seven-thirty in the morning! I serve my $@#%!! country for twenty-three $@#%!! years and this is what I get? You can't do this, you $@#%!! $@#%!!!"

A woman came out, a station employee. She tried to make peace between the two men, which is when I realized that the one who was checking the tickets was the driver of my bus. He knew that he had three seats, so he let those people on. He was going to step aboard and check for two more seats before he let us on.

Instead, he shrugged. "I don't have to take you," he said, walking away. He got on the bus, started the engine, and then drove out of the bus terminal.

Leaving me, an innocent bystander, standing in shocked silence behind an angry veteran who continued screaming and threatening violence. Everyone in the terminal was staring.

The station employee looked at me sympathetically. "You'll have to take the next bus. It leaves at six a.m." I stared at her, uncomprehending. Then I looked out the door, as if the bus driver was going to come back and say, "Sorry, I forgot that other lady." He did not.

"Don't worry, I'll make sure you get on the next one," said the woman, consolingly. I walked back to the seating area in a daze. I was devastated and desperately wanted to cry.

It was only eleven p.m. I was going to have to sit in this dreadful bus terminal all night.

To add to the indignity, a crew of cleaners propped open all the doors, and the temperature plummeted. Then they told the passengers to move out of the way, and they crammed all the benches together, so they could clean the floors.

That's when I ended up sitting next to the man in white, whom I'd noticed on my first bus. We smiled at each other wryly.

"Did you just come from work?" I asked. I thought perhaps he worked in a restaurant or a hospital. He looked puzzled by my question and answered no. "But I thought — your outfit —" I stammered, afraid that I had embarrassed him and was now embarrassing myself. He said something I didn't quite catch, and when I asked him to repeat it, he shook his head sadly and pantomimed taking a drink. I guessed he meant he'd just gotten out of rehab, so I didn't probe further.

As the cleaning crew started up loud floor-polishing machines, my conversation with the man in white grew organically. We compared notes about where we were heading, and how long our trips would take. He was going to "a town so small, you've probably never heard of it." He went on to explain that the closest town was Gastonia, but he had another long layover in Charlotte and wouldn't arrive until 6 pm. Given that I had seen him board the bus at about 8 pm, that meant over 22 hours to travel only 250 miles.

I told him I lived on a boat, and he admitted he'd never set foot on a boat. "I only been fishin' once." When he asked where I was going, I told him to Florida, and from there to Brazil. He'd never been out of the country in his life.

There was a long, comfortable silence, during which we watched the floor cleaners and a trio of 20-somethings across from us who were behaving erratically.

I asked him how long he'd be staying where he was going. "Oh, I'm going home," he said. Another silence, then I asked how long he'd been away.

His answer spoke volumes: "90 days."

Most people would say three months, or maybe "since October." A few days later, I confirmed my suspicion about his answer by running a search on the internet. There is a state mental hospital in Goldsboro. People who are involuntarily admitted cannot be kept longer than 90 days.

As the night wore on, people around us began grumbling about the cold. I got out a fleece jacket and draped it over my lap. My companion didn't complain, but I could tell he was chilled and had no jacket. I handed him a fleece quillow — a small blanket that converts to a pillow — and suggested that he could use it to keep warm. He accepted it gratefully.

We finally introduced ourselves after we'd been talking comfortably for a couple of hours. "By the way, I'm Thomas," he said, holding out his hand and chuckling. "I'm Margaret," I answered, shaking it like we'd just met. With the purple blanket around his shoulders, he looked like an Indian mystic.

After a while, we talked more than we were silent. He wanted to know about the boat and how it operated. Did it have a kitchen and a bathroom? Did I help steer it? Where had we gone in the boat? I asked questions about his family, what places he'd been to, what places he wanted to see. I even got out my laptop to show him photos of Alaska and Yukon, so he could see the beautiful light at midnight on the summer solstice.

Meanwhile, the mood in the bus terminal had gotten ugly. The veteran whose outburst had caused my bus driver to leave was — obviously — waiting for the same bus as me. He erupted every hour or so, yelling belligerently about how unfair this was, then settling down until something set him off again. The 20-somethings also got into repeated altercations with each other and with the employees. The good part was, it got quiet when they went outside to smoke. The bad part was, whatever they were smoking made them more volatile and more hostile when they came back. From the sores on their faces, I suspected methamphetamines.

It would have been terrifying, except that Thomas was very calm. His influence kept me calm, too.

With the purple blanket around his shoulders, he looked like an Indian mystic.

Sometime after three am, the floor cleaners began moving the benches back, and we had to move again. Thomas picked up my big purple suitcase, all 55 pounds of it, and we found a new spot that was agreeable to both of us. It was a given that we would continue to sit together as long as we were both in the terminal.

A while after that, they announced Thomas' bus. I stood up with him, and we said a reluctant farewell. We even exchanged a little hug, each hoping that our paths might cross again someday.

Across the terminal, I watched him waiting patiently in line, the blanket around his shoulders and the plastic bag in his hand. He was standing directly behind the group of obnoxious 20-somethings when things hit the fan.

For the first time all night, the 20-somethings wound up beside the volatile veteran. Like a match to tinder, they set each other off and then banded together against the employees. Suddenly, they were all shouting. The veteran began threatening to beat up the floor cleaners, shoving benches around, and lunging at them. The female employees were trying to placate them, to calm them down, but several of the male employees had reached their limits and were ready to get into fisticuffs with the passengers.

Thomas melted back against the wall, making himself invisible. That's when the police arrived. They took the difficult passengers outside, and everyone breathed a sigh of relief at the sudden quiet. Then Thomas and about 20 other people boarded the bus to Charlotte, and the room became quiet, half-empty.

I had to wait a few more hours for my bus, and when we boarded, the driver looked twice at my ticket. "You were supposed to be on the 11 pm bus," he told me. I just stared at him, afraid he was telling me I wasn't eligible for this bus, either. Then he waved me on. I climbed up the steps and looked down the aisle. Every seat was full but one, beside a Greyhound employee in the front row. She reluctantly moved her bags from my seat.

I had come so close to missing this bus that as we pulled out of the station, I burst into tears. The woman beside me turned to the window and ignored me.

When my sobs subsided, I found myself thinking of Thomas, my mysterious angel in white. I wondered what the future held for him in "a town so small, you've probably never heard of it." What tragic circumstances had caused him to go away for 90 days? In a small town, it would be hard to avoid the harsh judgments of family and neighbors. He would need all the patience I'd witnessed in him.

During that long, tough night in the Raleigh bus terminal, we'd both suspended our judgment of each other and found common ground. Based on appearances, he probably initially judged me and thought I wasn't much like him.

But I was. At that time, I was shaken by the fear that I was losing my mind, that I belonged in a place like the mental hospital in Goldsboro.

What story had Thomas written in his head about me, when he first got on the bus? Had he even noticed me, or had he been too engrossed in his reading and the question of what would be waiting on the other end of his journey? Once we had talked, what did he think of my real story, the one I shared in all those hours of conversation in the freezing-cold bus terminal? Had I communicated enough for him to really understand me?

Thomas would never know how valuable his kindness and calm companionship were to me. But perhaps the purple blanket would remind him that he had one friend out there in the world, a stranger named Margaret, who set aside judgment and spent time getting to know the real Thomas. Out there in the world, he had a friend who not only accepted him, but who genuinely liked and needed him.

CHAPTER 5

FACING DANGER
(BECAUSE I HAD NO OTHER CHOICE)

"You know that book you're writing? I don't think you could have those experiences with strangers in this day and age," said my brother, Dave.

"What do you mean?" I asked him, curious.

"Well, there was that woman whose car broke down, and when she knocked on a door to ask for help…"

"…the guy shot her. That one?" I completed his sentence.

Dave nodded, then went on to list several other recent incidents where people had done harm to harmless strangers.

The first thing I think about this sort of thing is that it vindicates my choice not to own or watch television. Television news thrives on drama, so the story about the woman getting shot has been repeated over and over. But what about all those people whose cars broke down, and they knocked on someone's door, used their phone to call AAA, and the news media never heard a peep about it? For every bad incident, there are probably hundreds of thousands of good ones, but they go unreported because there's no drama involved.

With that said, sometimes my interactions with strangers do carry a threat of violence or physical harm. When it can't be

*...and many other items that I
don't recall but would be glad
to have in an emergency.*

avoided, I take a deep breath, face my fear, and listen to my intuition. If I walk away unscathed — and so far, I always have — I end up with deep insight and a pretty amazing story to share.

When I was getting ready for my solo cross-country trip, my mother-in-law, Sharon, helped me pack. When it comes to being prepared, Sharon is the ultimate Girl Scout. She carries a capacious purse loaded with things like band-aids, emergency rations, safety pins, a rain bonnet, a screwdriver, tweezers, tissues, and many other items that I don't recall but would be glad to have in an emergency someday. Her wallet always has the right number of bills and coins to make change for any denomination.

As she helped me gather a few snacks and beverages, a knife, bowl, and fork, Sharon kept her opinions to herself. I told her that although I was going to be camping, I specifically didn't want to cook. At most, I wanted to be able to throw together a sandwich or salad.

This was quite a bit different from the camping trips she was used to, where everything the family needed to prepare a meal, eat it, and clean up was packed neatly into boxes. When they traveled, there was no need or desire to go to a restaurant or even to pick up an additional item at the country store. The family was a completely self-sufficient unit.

This was the opposite of what I wanted.

I knew I did not want to be self-sufficient. Self-sufficiency would isolate me from the places I passed through. I wanted an excuse to go into every grocery, restaurant, convenience store, or country market. I wanted to ask people in neighboring campsites or cottages for salt or catsup.

But asking for sugar — that's a whole 'nuther story, which illustrates just how stupidly naive I can be.

I had rented a cottage in Chincoteague, Virginia for a week. I spent my days alone, writing, exploring the little town on foot, and looking for wild ponies at the nearby Assateague Island Wildlife Refuge.

Near the end of my week, there was a knock on the back door. When I opened it, there was a man I hadn't seen before standing there, and he asked me if I had any sugar. He seemed very curious about the layout of my cottage, peering over my shoulder into the interior.

I shook my head and told him I only had some artificial sweetener. "What's it for?" I asked.

He kind of stammered and mumbled, then he asked me, directly, "Are you alone?"

It turned out that he and his friend, who were living in the next two cottages and working at a nearby NASA facility, didn't really need any sugar. That was just the excuse to check out the good-looking lady next door and see if she really was single. "We're cooking some dinner on the barbecue. Do you want to eat with us?"

I took in the picnic table and the grill and thought the invitation seemed innocuous enough. "Sure, that sounds like fun," I said.

What I didn't realize was that although they were grilling the meat outside, it was a chilly October evening, and the table was set inside.

The fellow who had invited me was a pilot named Alex. His co-worker and companion, an aeronautical engineer named Greg, was doing all the cooking, including three kinds of grilled meats, vegetables, potatoes, and salad. There was enough food for about eight people, and enough alcohol for twenty.

I made it clear that although my husband was not with me, I was married and not interested in anything other than food and conversation. Greg, who was single, took me at my word. Alex, who was married, tried to convince me to sleep with him. Evidently, this was what he meant when he had asked me earlier if I had any "sugar."

Over the course of the evening, Alex drank heavily and became too loaded to make sense. He kept trying to convince me that I should sleep with him because he was a jet pilot and made a lot of money. Greg rolled his eyes, trying unsuccessfully to keep his friend from embarrassing himself.

When Alex wasn't interrupting us, Greg and I found lots of interesting things to talk about.

We talked about flying and sailing and family and religion. We talked about the cemetery that was next door, and whether there were ghosts there. Even though he was an engineer, a man of science, Greg was too superstitious to walk around in a graveyard after dark.

On the other hand, I was not only willing to walk around in a cemetery after dark, I really wanted to go over there and see what it was like.

"You're a crazy lady!" said the drunken Alex, who'd been unable to follow the conversation until that point. "I would never, ever, uh..." he forgot what he was saying and started picking at his food again.

Greg didn't have strong ties to a particular church, but he was a devout Christian who relied strongly on his faith in Jesus and God. He seemed dismayed when I said that I didn't have that kind of faith. He wasn't trying to convert me, but all evening long, the conversation kept coming back to faith.

Greg admitted that he felt no fear around airplanes, even skydiving or flying aboard experimental aircraft, but the thought of being on a boat out of sight of land frightened him. He told me the story of a boating accident on the Mississippi river that he'd barely survived. He described what it was like to nearly drown, and how he'd tried unsuccessfully to save his teenaged nephew.

"I'm sorry," I said, and we shared a moment of silence at the tragic loss of a young life.

Greg was worried about my plans to sail across the Atlantic Ocean aboard our 33-foot boat, *Flutterby*. "When you go out on that little tiny boat, out of sight of land, aren't you scared? All kinds of terrible things could happen! What makes you think you'll be safe?"

I thought carefully about the question, and about what he'd said earlier about his religion.

"I do have faith," I told him. "It's just a different kind."

He chuckled. "Wow. I guess you do."

Then Alex, who had been sleeping drunkenly with his face on the table, woke with a snort. He looked up at me with glazed eyes and the remains of his dinner on his chin. "I think I love you," he slurred. "Wanna fuck?"

I survived the evening without harm, because Greg was a gentleman and a genuinely kind person who would look out for me. Besides, his companion was too drunk to do anything but use his potty-mouth to give me a really bad impression of airplane pilots. Neither one of them was brave enough to follow me into the graveyard after dark.

Greg is not the only stranger who has looked out for me. Barry and I once had a whole subway-car full of silent strangers looking out for us.

We were returning to Lisbon after a couple of weeks exploring Portugal by train and bus. Wearing our large backpacks, we boarded a too-crowded subway train at rush hour. We only had to travel about five stops to the center of town, but at the first stop, it happened.

I looked across the crowded car at Barry and noticed that the camera bag, which he had across his shoulder, was unzipped. About the same time, someone standing next to him caught my eye and pointed out the same thing, silently. Several people pointed to the train doors, which were closing. They didn't say anything, just pointed to the platform.

Stolen? I couldn't believe it! Without looking to see what Barry was doing, I leaped for the subway door, which was closing. It got caught on my backpack and then sprang back open.

I staggered onto the silent platform and looked to my right. There was no one there. To my left, two men were about to head up the stairs. I shouted something — I don't know

The subway doors bounced off my backpack.

what — and a kind elderly gentleman looked over his shoulder at my frantic face. He pointed to the younger man ahead of him. Silently.

Fired by adrenaline and rage, I ran up to the stairs and grabbed the man he had pointed to, spinning him around to face me. "Where's my camera? I want my camera!" I shouted in his face. He shrugged, the classic "I don't know" gesture. Just then, Barry came pelting down the platform.

Wedged in the crowd of people, Barry wouldn't have made it off the train and would have gone on to the next station, except that the doors had bounced off my backpack. He slid through as they were about to close a second time.

Thinking the camera was around the man's neck, Barry grabbed his jacket, and the man didn't even resist.

That's because the camera wasn't around his neck. He was too smart for that. Not smart enough, though.

He'd stuck it down his sleeve. Luckily for us, in his haste, the lens cap had come off and was dangling by a small cord from his armpit. Barry pulled on it, and out came our precious new — three weeks old — camera.

We just stared at the thief, and he shrugged again and walked away without saying anything. The sound of his footsteps echoed down the platform as we sat and waited for the next train. The adrenaline rush had subsided, leaving me weak-kneed and very, very grateful for the strangers who had looked out for us.

Who were those kindly people who had pointed out the thief and made sure we got our camera back? And why were they all silent?

The lens cap was dangling by a small cord from his armpit.

The scariest stranger I ever talked to was a man name Darren. The reason I talked with him for almost an hour was simply because I was so terrified of him and any gang members who might have been in the neighborhood.

It was on Mardi Gras day, in New Orleans, a couple of years before Hurricane Katrina.

At seven o'clock in the morning, Barry and I had driven across town to watch the Zulu parade. We found a parking space near the freeway; it wasn't very close to the parade, but we were happy to walk the streets and soak up the excitement. Everyone was out and about, preparing for the big day. Even though the houses had backyards, most of the barbecue grills and tables were being set up in the front yards. Some people were even putting them on the grassy medians in the middle of the street, in order to share the feast with neighbors on the other side.

Zulu, the traditionally black parade, had a wonderful energy, different from the ones we'd watched earlier in the week. Afterwards, we watched a couple more parades, walking further and further away from where we'd parked our car. It was afternoon before we returned, our backpack full of silly Mardi Gras throws from the parades, mostly beads and plastic cups.

As we left the residential neighborhood and turned down the street to the car, I realized that things had changed a lot in a few hours. Now our little Honda sat forlornly in the middle of a bunch of abandoned, boarded-up warehouses. All the other cars and people were gone. As we approached the car, a belligerent young man confronted us. He wore baggy pants and was carrying something in a paper bag.

His manner terrified me. I was afraid that his clothing concealed a weapon, and that we were about to be robbed, or beaten. The only approach I could think of was to disarm him with friendliness. Surely he wouldn't harm someone who was nice to him?

So I gave him a big smile. "Hi! How're you doing today?"

It worked, but not in the way I expected. The man was definitely taken aback.

"You guys are undercover cops, aren't you?" he said.

Now it was my turn to be taken aback. "No, no, not us."

He insisted that we were undercover cops, because what would we be doing in this dangerous neighborhood otherwise?

So began a very strange encounter, where we spent the better part of an hour telling him about ourselves, trying to convince him that we were not undercover cops. He spent that time telling us about himself, trying to convince us that we shouldn't arrest him.

It was an amazing glimpse into another world.

The man, whose name was Darren, showed us his parole card. He showed us the receipts that proved he'd paid his child support. He showed us his bullet wounds, both the entrance and the exit scars. He showed us what was in the paper bag — a bottle of Thunderbird 20/20.

"If you're not a cop, then take a drink," he demanded.

The funny thing was, Darren simply did not want us to leave. He just wanted to talk and talk and talk. At first, he stood between us and our car. Then he sat on the hood. When I unlocked the door and got into the driver's seat, he literally sat on the running board at my feet, so I couldn't drive away.

At first, I didn't want to brush him off because I was so scared. He was so belligerent, his manner so full of restrained violence, that I was afraid he would take revenge. As the surreal encounter continued, I realized that Darren wasn't a threat, but that he was desperate to be heard, and he didn't want us to abandon him. By then my fear had turned to compassion, and strangely enough, I simply stayed because I didn't want to hurt his feelings.

It was probably 30 minutes into the encounter before he was convinced we weren't cops. He changed his tactics.

"OK, if you're not cops, then what do you want? I can get you drugs, sex…you want a threesome?" He continued at length, telling us what kinds of illicit things he could procure on our behalf.

It took another 10 minutes to convince him that we didn't want anything illicit. Bewildered and disappointed, he asked us for a ride downtown. We pointed out that we didn't have room in the car for a third person, so he was down to his last resort, asking us to give him money.

Darren showed us his bullet wounds.

Still, Darren had some pride, and he was no beggar. At some point, he stood up from the running board of the little Honda, and I closed the door and started the engine.

"We have to go now, Darren," I said, firmly, as I drove away.

About a block and a half down the street, a man on the sidewalk gestured to get our attention, and I rolled down my window. "Your friend back there wants you," he said. I looked in the rearview mirror to see Darren waving his arms and shouting at us as we drove away.

"If you're not a cop, then take a drink."

"Thank you, I know," I said, shaking my head sadly.

I turned the corner, taking a slightly different route back to the freeway, and was completely shocked. The place where we had parked the car was adjacent to the saddest, most derelict blocks of housing projects I'd ever seen.

I caught a rare glimpse into American urban poverty that day. Driving past the housing projects, I saw garbage and decay and neglected children playing in the dirt. Before that day, I could barely have imagined the kind of desperate people who lived there. Thanks to Darren, I had a name and a face to help me understand the cycle of poverty and the violence that accompanies it.

My initial fear of Darren, my fear that he was carrying a weapon and would hurt me, was minimal and short-lived compared to the fear and desperation he and his neighbors live with every day. My life is easy and safe compared to his. Looking back, I suspect that he was more scared of me than I was of him. At least, as long as he thought I was an undercover cop.

I emerged unscathed from my frightening experience with Darren on Mardi Gras day. Unscathed, but not unchanged.

CHAPTER 6

WHAT'S THE WORST THING
THAT CAN HAPPEN?

I know there are psychopaths out there in the world, and I might run into one. I haven't run into one yet, so I tend to believe that the odds are low. For me, it's worth taking the risk.

Leaving aside psychopaths, there are other people who might try to take advantage of me in smaller ways. Here, I apply some cost-benefit analysis. How many strangers am I going to meet who will subtract from my life, and how many will add to it?

Encounters with strangers have added much to my life, and have rarely subtracted anything. Some encounters are a net zero, like the one where Barry and I ended up with the same amount of pocket change, and beer, that we started out with.

We were sitting in the front seat of the Squid Wagon, parked next to Lake Union, in Seattle. We'd just returned from an afternoon boat ride aboard *Flagrante Delicto*, skippered by the notorious Captain Craig, Scourge of Lake Union and Environs.

A man rode by on an old-style single-speed bicycle. He caught my eye, because unlike most Seattle cyclists, he wasn't wearing a helmet or a backpack. A few minutes later, he circled back and knocked on the driver's window. Barry rolled it down, and the man said, "I

"I can't lie. I was going to use it for beer."

need to catch a bus, but I don't have enough change. Do you have 57 cents?"

Reluctantly, Barry said, "I guess so." Then he reached for the little handful of change we keep in the van, while the man rooted around in his pockets. "Uh, wait a minute, I thought I had more here," said the guy. "I guess I need a dollar fifty."

Barry handed him the change we had and said, "Here's five quarters. You'll have to get the rest from someone else."

"Thanks," said the man, taking the money. He hesitated for a moment, as if he was going to ask for something else, but Barry rolled the window up. The guy got the hint and rode away.

A few minutes later, he was back, tapping at the window. "I can't lie," he said. "I was going to use this for beer. Do you want it back?"

Barry said, "Yeah," and to my surprise, the man simply handed him back the five quarters. "Next time, ask for the beer first, man," said Barry.

The guy nodded earnestly and said, "OK, sorry." He paused, but he didn't leave. Then, "Can I have some money for beer?"

Barry was indignant. 'No, I said next time, ask for the beer first!" But he was smiling as he rolled up the window again, and the man shrugged and left.

Barry sat in the driver's seat, staring incredulously at the handful of change that he'd given as a handout and then had returned. That's when we both burst out laughing, and we couldn't stop. Although we don't like beer, we actually *had* some with us — lots of it!

"If he'd said first off that beer was what he wanted, instead of money, I would have given him plenty!" said Barry.

One time, there was a guy I wish we hadn't talked to. We called him Chicken Pox Man.

We were unable to control the man's choice of conversational topics.

I was cooking breakfast in a public park in Bangor, Maine, when he walked by and struck up a conversation. He was nondescript, indeterminate age, but friendly and garrulous, just a local fellow out taking a walk around the neighborhood.

Barry and I had parked the Squid Wagon nearby and carried our stove, cooking implements, and food to a public picnic table. We were a captive audience, because we had all that stuff spread out on the table, where we were chopping fresh vegetables and sauteeing them. We couldn't carry all of it in one load, and besides, the stove was hot.

It would have been fine, except we were unable to control the man's choice of conversational topics.

He very deliberately brought it around to a subject near and dear to his heart: A meticulous, explicit description of the life-threatening case of chicken pox he had suffered as a teenager. Like a freight train, he gathered steam and just kept talking in great detail about the horrific experience. No gentle conversational cues could stop him from describing the rectal exam he received as a result of his condition!

I was ready to chew my own leg off to escape. It went from strange to boring to simply dreadful. It was so dreadful that later, we found it funny. As the years go by, and the details of the rectal exam fade in my mind, it seems much funnier.

Chicken Pox Man was, hands-down, the worst encounter I've ever had with a stranger.

It seems trivial, but one of the things that hurts the most is rejection. It's happened to me a few times. More than a few times.

Being rebuffed feels bad, for a little while. But a truly elegant rejection can be memorable. It's like the time I bought a box of candy called "Gummy Boogers" to share with my friends. Nobody actually wanted to eat the gross green things, but a year later, that's the only thing we remember from *that* camping trip.

When Barry and I were exploring Newfoundland with my father, we parked our van in a remote gravel lot overlooking the ocean and went on a short hike. The Squid Wagon was the only vehicle in the lot

"It's not allowed."

when we departed, but when we returned, there was a truck parked beside it.

We'd been in Newfoundland long enough to have gotten used to the super-friendly local folks, so Dad walked over to say hello to the bearded man in flannel. He was sitting on a park bench, looking out at the ocean.

"It's a beautiful day for fishing, isn't it?" said Dad.

"Can't fish," said the man, flatly, without looking at him.

"Are you a fisherman?" persisted Dad.

"You can't fish," the man repeated.

Dad started to ask a third question, but the man just scowled at him and said, "It's not allowed." He probably meant fishing, but we took it to mean asking him questions. We quickly got into the van and drove away, leaving him alone with his thoughts.

I won't forget the sight of that bitter man, alone on his park bench, gazing out at an ocean that was forbidden to him after a lifetime of fishing. His brush-off gave the collapse of the cod fisheries a sad, human face.

CHAPTER 7

BETTER THAN GOOGLE

I was soaking in my favorite hot pool, the one at the Symes Hotel in Hot Springs, Montana. This time, I was traveling without Barry, and there were three women I'd never met in the pool with me. Two of them were elderly, and had driven down from Canada to "take the waters" for their health. One was beautiful and graceful in the water, but was bent nearly double, staggering with crippling arthritis on land. Her friend, who did the driving, used the trip as an excuse to hunt for bargains in U.S. antique stores.

The third woman was quite young, a Millenial hippie who said she had been living in her van when she landed in Hot Springs and couldn't think of a better place to go. She found a couple of part-time jobs, saved her money, and finally rented an apartment.

"My landlord thinks I'm crazy, because I'm still living in my van. In the driveway," she said. She glared at me defiantly, as if daring me to call her crazy, too. I just nodded politely without saying anything.

I had my own crazy story. A little while later, after the three of us had been chatting about a wide variety of topics, I mentioned that I

West

East

was doing an unusual research project as I drove across the country by myself. I was looking for the Butter Divide.

I've lived on both the east coast and the west coast of the USA, as well as in the middle. I love to bake cookies for my friends, and I've done that on both coasts, too. Real homemade cookies, made with real butter.

As a result, I noticed that up and down the east coast, and as far west as Ohio, butter quarters, or sticks, are long and skinny. In Washington and Oregon, they are short and fat. The weight is the same — a quarter pound. Because the packaging is different, some butter dishes are skinny and some are fat. Some are big enough to allow for either shape.

I began to obsess on a simple question: Where is the line, in the middle of the United States, where the butter quarters change from being skinny to being fat? In other words, where is the Butter Divide?

When I explained this to the women in the hot pool, the results were mixed. The woman with arthritis nodded politely, but had nothing to say about it. Her friend, the antique-lover, became quite animated, talking excitedly about how you could research the historical shape of butter dishes to figure it out.

The young, intense one interrupted her. She told me, flatly, that I should do my research on the Internet.

"You should Google it," she said.

I pointed out that would defeat the purpose of my trip, which was to talk with strangers, and she rolled her eyes. "She's on a quest," she said to the other two, sarcastically. "What a waste of time."

I began to obsess on a simple question.

We had a basic difference of opinion: I don't *ever* consider talking with strangers to be a waste of my time.

It's great to have resources, to be able to get my own answers on the internet, to be able to take care of myself. The problem is, that can isolate me. If I don't need other people, I don't have an excuse, however small, to interact with them. Being too self-sufficient can get lonely.

If I start feeling overly proud of my self-sufficiency — "See? I can do everything myself!" — I get a double penalty. Now, not only do I not need to talk with people, but when I do, I am an insufferable bore.

Barry isn't shy, but he talks with fewer strangers than I do. He is extremely self-sufficient, just like his mother, and darned proud of it. When we were living aboard *Flutterby* in Brunswick, Georgia, without a car, our marina neighbor offered to give us a ride to the grocery store. "No thanks," said Barry, cheerfully, "it's only a three-mile walk." I kicked him.

The next time I ran into that neighbor, I gladly accepted a ride. I learned a lot about him and my other neighbors and the goings-on in the marina in those few short blocks! Barry was doing a lot of walking, but he was also missing out on some great candy from strangers.

Sometimes, though, the tables get turned, and he shows me how it's done.

We were exploring the neighborhood around our marina, and we discovered a strip mall with a variety store and an auto-parts store. I was meandering towards the variety store, but Barry made a beeline for the auto-parts store. Since we were holding hands, his beeline overruled my meander.

"Wait a minute," I protested. "What do we need there?"

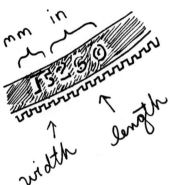

"You could have Googled that…but I'm glad you didn't!"

"A spare alternator belt," he said. Then he admitted, "But I don't know what size."

I stopped on the sidewalk in front of the store, before he could drag me through the door. "You'll just be wasting their time," I pointed out. "You need to measure the belt first."

"I've looked at it," said Barry, "but the markings don't say what size it is."

"Can't you look in the manual?" I was particularly stubborn that day, but Barry's persistence and momentum won the argument. I reluctantly followed him into the auto-parts store.

The place was empty, and the lone employee behind the counter greeted us eagerly with, "How can I help you?"

"I need a spare alternator belt for my boat engine," said Barry, "but there are so many numbers on it, I don't know which one identifies the size."

"What kind of boat?" the man asked. When we told him we lived aboard a sailboat, he wanted to hear more. Where were we from? Where were we docked? Where had we sailed? For about ten minutes, he gave us a wealth of local knowledge about marinas and auto parts stores and other places to get boat parts. Finally, the conversation wound back around to the alternator belt.

"Here, let me show you how to read it, so you don't have to take it off the engine," said the employee. He got a couple of alternator belts from the parts area and brought them out to us. "See, these first two digits are the width of the belt in millimeters. It's usually 13, 15, or 17. The other three digits are the length, in inches. So 15260 is 15 millimeters wide and 26 inches around."

"Seriously?" asked Barry.

Having a 5-digit number comprised of a width in millimeters and a circumference in inches seemed so silly that the three of us started laughing. I felt like I'd been admitted to a special club of people who understand the code of alternator belts.

We were still chuckling as we left the store. On the sidewalk, Barry asked me. "See? Aren't you glad we went in there?"

"You know, you probably could have Googled that..." He stopped to look at me in dismay, then noticed that I was grinning at him. "...but I'm glad you didn't. That was fun!"

It was another reminder that being self-sufficient is not the best way to get candy. Having a need or a question — in the case of the auto-parts store, having both — gives us an excuse to talk to strangers.

That's one of the reasons I don't like to carry detailed maps. When I started driving from Seattle to North Carolina alone, in 2009, I didn't have a smartphone, and there were only a few maps in the car — Washington, Nevada, Utah. I'd be driving through at least 15 other states, and I wouldn't even need Nevada or Utah, since I was taking a northern route! I was deliberately setting off without the maps I needed.

Without a map or a GPS, I had a reason to ask for directions. I could ask strangers where to go, get suggestions from them about the best route or campground or ice cream shop.

Sometimes, on that trip, I didn't even know where I was. Then I had the perfect conversational opener. I had an excuse to ask, "I know I am 'here,' but can you tell me where 'here' is?"

My stomach was grumbling with hunger as I drove along Highway 87, a two-lane road in Montana. There was nothing to see but ranchland, so when I saw a cafe advertising breakfast burritos, I stopped.

There is a moment of suspense when I open the door to an establishment with super-dark, tinted windows. Will it be dark and dirty inside, full of cigarette smoke and men staring at me as I open the door? Will I regret this? I fought down my fear and pushed the door open.

Mr. Stetson

To my surprise, it was a bright and cheerful cafe, with an efficient, friendly waitress. The first time she refilled my coffee cup, she moved so silently that I jumped. "Sorry," she said. "No, it's OK," I replied. "You're like a coffee angel."

Two men sat down at the next table. The older one wore a baseball cap. The younger one's head was bare. They were joined by a third man, between them in age and wearing a Stetson.

The three of them gazed out the window, talking about the people driving by on the highway. Their conversation was roundabout, slow, disjointed.

"He flies here every week from Great Falls," said the older one.

"Really? Why?" asked the middle one.

"His plane only does 95," said the young one.

"For lunch, I guess."

"He buys a new car every six months."

"Is that thing she drives a car or a truck?"

"Both, I think."

A tinny song interrupted their conversation. The two older men fell silent and drank their coffee while the young man answered his phone. He talked so loudly that everyone in the restaurant could not only hear him, but couldn't tune him out. "I dunno, it's my birthday...Hey, I gotta go, I got another call...Hi, Dad...I'm here with Grandpa...Naw, 21 doesn't feel any different."

The kid finally hung up his phone, and the three of them resumed their conversation, talking about how to ultrasound a cow. Mr. Stetson had a technique that Grandpa Baseball Cap was interested in.

Grandpa Baseball Cap

"We did 370 in one day; I've done 240 by myself," said Stetson.

"Why?" asked the kid.

"To figure out the carcass quality before they're dead," said Stetson.

I interrupted their conversation briefly. "Excuse me, can you tell me the name of this town?"

The three looked at each other, surprised, and then Stetson answered. "Stanford," he said. "...Montana." We all laughed. We were not only many miles from the next town, we were hundreds of miles from any other state.

"There's a $25 fine for asking," he said.

I once spent a few weeks traveling with a sailor named Steve and his wife, Judy. He was the most curious person I had ever met, absolutely full of guileless questions. Steve would simply walk up to people, get in their faces, and start asking them rapid-fire questions. "What are you doing?" "Why are you using that tool?" "Where does this road go?" "What kind of fish is that?" "Do you know where you're going, and can I follow you?" The one that made Judy and me cringe was, "If you're throwing that away, can I have it?"

I'm a little more shy than Steve about asking direct questions. Nonetheless, I love to put myself into situations where I don't know what's going on, so I have an excuse to ask questions, even stupid ones.

One recent Saturday morning, I had a chance to practice this in Brunswick, Georgia. I'd walked over to the farmers' market, but instead of a few vendors with vegetables and fruit, I happened upon several thousand people milling around the park. It was a traditional city-wide event, the Brunswick Rockin' Stewbilee. The highlight of the event was the stew-tasting, 35 booths offering a sample of the stew that was named for this small city.

Or was it? One of the first people I questioned was a woman who told me, "We do this every year, because Brunswick stew was named after Brunswick." She laughed. "But it might have been named after Brunswick County, Virginia. They make a lot of stew up there, too."

"It's the fruitcake of stew," said a young man in a chef's hat, in response to my next question. He was stirring a gigantic pot over a propane burner. His companions from the Altamaha Technical College Culinary Arts program laughed at his answer, but they all nodded their agreement.

I asked the young man in the chef's hat, "What's in it?"

"Chicken, pork, beef, lima beans, corn, potatoes, tomatoes, spices… it's a fridge-cleaning stew."

At that point, I decided to talk to more chefs and find out whose fridge they were cleaning out. I walked up to a couple of guys and asked them, "I heard this is fridge-cleaning stew. If so, whose fridge are you cleaning out?"

"That would be mine, I guess," said Tom, a retiree from the pulp mill who was on the "stew crew" of the hospital auxiliary. When he worked for the pulp mill, his employer used his recipe in the competition, but he had switched his loyalty to the hospital after retirement. The pulp mill had to come up with a different recipe.

It was a lively competition. When you purchased a ticket, you were given two votes to cast for the People's Choice award. There was also a Judge's award, selected by local celebrities, and a Presentation Award. The teams represented restaurants, local businesses, clubs, and even a few dedicated families who wanted to feed stew to hundreds of people.

One local business was giving away schwag with their samples. "Are you trying to bribe the voters?" I asked. "Oh, no, ma'am, I would not stoop that low!" said the volunteer. He turned to hand a stew sample and a Frisbee to a woman, saying, "Here, go taste that and then come back and give me your vote."

I made my way around the booths, looking for the trophies indicating previous award-winners. One group, from the Ole Times Country Buffet, had several 2nd- and 3rd-place trophies. They were attracting a lot of attention by making the most noise in the place, ringing ear-splitting cowbells every time someone tasted or voted for their stew.

"We tried that last year," said a woman from the hospital auxiliary. "It backfired on us, and we didn't get as many votes as the year before." When I cast my vote for Tom's recipe, she picked up a cowbell and rang it rather gingerly. "There's a sleeping baby behind you," she said, by way of explanation.

I wandered from one booth to the next, tasting and asking questions, trying to figure out what made an award-winning Brunswick stew. More than one person told me, "It's about balancing the flavors." Among the samples I tried, the chicken, pork, and tomatoes were consistent, but the flavors ranged from sweet to salty to spicy to bland. The top award-winner, from a group called Re-

"It's a tablespoon of happiness…"

nessenz, was the sweetest one I tasted, and I suspected their secret ingredient was sugar.

I later looked up Renessenz, to see what the company did, and decided that if they had a secret ingredient, I didn't want to know what it was. "Renessenz LLC is the leading producer of terpene-based aroma chemicals," said their slick website.

The truth is, the secret ingredient in Brunswick stew isn't really a secret. When I asked, everyone was proud to tell me their "secret": "Tender-loving care," "You know how Grandmother used to cook? That's my secret." The county commissioners admitted that they didn't cook the stew, their staff did. "Our secret is teamwork."

The simplest, best secret ingredient was that of Gateway Behavioral Health Services, a group that had won many awards over the years, including the People's Choice, the Judge's Award, and the Presentation Award. These folks had given their stew a name: Happy Stew.

"Love is the secret ingredient in our stew," said a volunteer named Jeff. When I pressed him for details, asking how they measured how much love to put in, he replied, "We measure it by the width of unicorn hairs, and the intensity of the dreams of pregnant mermaids."

Another volunteer, Barbara, chimed in, "It's a tablespoon of happiness…"

"No," said Jeff, "it's half a tablespoon. We were a little too happy last year, we had to cut it back. People started a drum circle, started playing Age of Aquarius, and we decided that was just a little too much for around here."

The Stewbilee gave me so many excuses to walk up to friendly strangers and ask questions, I changed my original plans and stayed for hours. That reminded me of another small-town event I'd stumbled upon, a few years earlier, where I had a chance to wander around, satisfying a life-long curiosity and asking "dumb" questions about trucks.

Barry were driving across Iowa on the interstate when a gigantic sign caught my eye. "World's Largest Truck Stop," it said. There was a huge traffic jam associated with the world's largest truck stop — the off-ramp was backed up with cars and semis. Such traffic jams are unheard of in a place where cows outnumber people.

At 65 mph, I had only an instant to decide. I switched off the cruise control and joined the traffic jam without consulting Barry.

The off-ramp was perched high above the truck stop, and we could see down into vast acres of trucks, cars, pedestrians, and — huh? Circus tents? What was going on at the world's largest truck stop?

It felt surreal to follow signs for overflow parking without knowing why. The Squid Wagon was directed to a field, about a half mile from the center of the activity. Just after we'd locked up and grabbed cameras and sun hats, an ancient yellow school bus came by and picked us up. Someone handed us a program, which said, "Welcome to the 31st Annual Walcott Truckers Jamboree." Bouncing on poor suspension across bumpy fields, the school bus delivered us to the entrance of what the program said was "The Best Trucker Party in the Country! FUN! for all."

On our many cross-country road
trips, Barry and I have always looked
at big trucks and asked each other
questions like, "What do you sup-
pose that thingie is for?" "Why is he
doing *that*?" "What do you think is
in *there*?" Since neither of us had ever
been inside a semi, we spent a lot of
time arguing about the possible answers without any real facts on which
to base our positions.

We call this sort of discussion
"talking out of our butts."

Finally, at the Jamboree, we could
get some answers, maybe even settle
an old argument or two. Just the
previous day, we'd debated this one:
Why do truckers pay to be weighed
at a truck stop, when state weigh sta-
tions do it for free?

The first exhibitor at the show, a

*Circus tents? What was going on at
the world's largest truck stop?*

representative of CAT Scales, answered that question easily — some
truckers want to make sure the weight of their load is legal before they
drive into a weigh station, where they will be fined if it's not. Also,
some loads, such as household goods, are charged by weight.

We wandered the big tent, where exhibitors were touting everything from dip mixes to air filters and 12-volt mattress warmers. One
driver had self-published a novel, but without an audio version, he
wasn't getting much interest from his fellow drivers. Trucking compa-
nies were handing out freebies to anyone with a CDL, hoping to re-
cruit drivers. The American Lung Association and the Iowa Soybean
Association, unrelated organizations with different interests, were
both pushing biodiesel. I stopped to look at literature for Women in
Trucking, and two women pounced on me as a potential member.
Later, when I read their newsletter, I realized I should have asked to
see their Women in Trucking tattoos.

We left the exhibits and started strolling through the rows of trucks, taking pictures of shiny chrome and elaborate airbrushed graphics. What was the story on these trucks? Were they for sale, or just for show? Who had brought them?

The acres of blacktop gave off waves of heat, and the only shade came from the trucks themselves. We came upon a small group in folding chairs, chatting animatedly in the shade between two trucks.

When questioned, they explained that they were owner-operators who came every year. I asked about their trucks, and one couple pointed to the one on the left, and the other pointed to the one on the right. "Are you staying in your trucks?" I asked. "We're staying in the hotel," answered one of the women. "But they're staying here. She has a real bathroom in hers, with a shower," she said, enviously. The sleeper on the truck with the bathroom was about three times larger than other sleepers, and had larger windows. It looked like a very sturdy RV.

In campgrounds, Barry and I had learned a little bit about RVers, many of whom are retirees who drive around the country and pay handsomely for the fuel to do so. The truckers had smaller accommodations but bigger rigs. "We get paid to do our traveling," said one of the women, proudly.

Yet their lives were spent on the road, barely crossing paths with their trucking friends. The Jamboree gave them an excuse to stop and relax together, on the pavement in the shade of their rigs. They could talk in person, instead of on the CB radio.

Another proud driver sat beside his shiny purple rig, which featured airbrushed white horses charging out of blue surf. The multitalented owner-operator had painted it himself. Not only that, but he'd built the interior of the sleeper from scratch. It was the only one we saw that included a tiny corner fireplace. We climbed up into the cab, with its hundreds of shiny buttons and switches, to see the sculpture on the back wall of the sleeper, a continuation of the horses in surf theme.

The same man told us we absolutely had to stay for the nighttime party. He went into rapture, describing the illuminated trucks in the Lights at Night Competition, and told us people would be walking around and admiring each others' trucks all night long. There would be a fireworks show and a concert by big-name country musician Tracy Lawrence. I had to take his word that Tracy Lawrence was famous, having never heard of him, myself.

I seriously considered his recommendation to stay. I felt very welcome, and we could easily have hung out all day and through the night, partying with the big truck people. But in the end, we decided to push on across Iowa and save our free time for places that were greener and cooler (and had better music).

We drove about 20 miles up the road and stopped at a rest area, where a man who was cleaning the restrooms struck up a conversation with me. He was a very overweight man, one of the largest I've ever seen, and admitted that he'd never been away from home. I sensed that working in a rest area made him restless, wishing to see more of the world. When I said that we'd just come from the big truck jamboree, his face lit up. "I'm going to that tomorrow," he told me.

I told him what I'd heard about the nighttime party, the fireworks and the music and the illuminated trucks, and he got more and more excited. "I won't wait until tomorrow," he said. "I get off at nine, so I'll just go over there tonight! Thanks for telling me!"

He pushed his cart across the rest area, beaming. Barry and I continued driving down the interstate, looking up at the big trucks, with a little more understanding of what was going on in the lives of their drivers.

Working in a rest area made him restless.

CHAPTER 8

WHEN RECEIVING IS A GIFT

The last time the Squid Wagon broke down, I was so embarrassed, I wished the pavement would swallow me up. Barry had his head stuck under the hood, troubleshooting the problem. I was the one directing traffic behind the van, facing the angry, frustrated drivers who were confronted with 7000 pounds of "dead squid" stuck squarely in the middle of a Seattle city street.

During a lull in the traffic, I walked up to the front of the van. "Can't we push it out of the road?" I asked Barry, forlornly. I was tired of people scowling at me. A few of them had even honked their horns! That's a sound rarely heard in Seattle, a city known for its super-polite residents.

"No, it's too heavy," he replied, and resumed his focused head-scratching.

A few minutes later, a couple of joggers came by, and to my surprise, they stopped. "Let's see what we can do," they said. The three of us put our shoulders against the back of the vehicle, and lo and behold, it moved! In less than two minutes, we pushed it to a safe place on the side of the road.

When I thanked them profusely, they said, ""We were out here to get exercise — we should thank you for giving us a better workout!"

That made me stop and think. How often do I refuse genuine offers of help? Simply receiving the gift of assistance and responding with a genuine "thank you" can make people feel good about themselves.

A couple of years earlier, on a cross-country road trip in the Squid Wagon, we were leaving my brother's driveway in Durham, North Carolina, when I heard a loud metallic THUNK from the rear of the van. "What was that?" I asked Barry. "That's the ladder, shifting," he said, "or maybe the camp stools. Or both." "OK," I said, and continued driving.

A sharpish corner brought another THUNK from the rear. I didn't think about it until the next one, THUNK, which was the turn onto the interstate on-ramp.

The THUNKs subsided, because there were no more sharp turns. But I began obsessively worrying, worrying, worrying. What was that metal ladder bumping into? Could it be the van's window? Would the next THUNK be accompanied by breaking glass?

I finally voiced my worries, along with the statement that "we" should do something about it. (By "we," of course, I meant Barry.)

"OK, next rest area," he said. From the look on his face, I knew he was engineering a solution to the problem. He was thinking so hard, I imagined I saw small smoke puffs coming out of his ears.

Around dusk, I stopped at a scenic overlook near Pilot Mountain. Barry had decided what to do: We'd stretch out the 12-foot ladder, strap a sausage-shaped bundle of fabric and pipe to that, and tie the

"We should thank you for giving us a better workout!"

whole mess to the roof rack. Since the Squid Wagon is 17 feet long, it wouldn't even stick out.

Barry lifted the folded ladder out of the back, and I breathed a sigh of relief. The window wasn't cracked. Then he passed it to me, saying "Make it flat," and my relief went away.

The darned Versaladder

We've had this Versaladder for years, and it hates me. It has four ladder segments and three sets of hinges, so it can be converted from stepladder to scaffold or tall ladder. No matter how hard I try to avoid it, the darned thing always pinches my fingers badly when I adjust it. This time, I was worrying so much about my fingers that a heavy, spring-loaded section of the gangly ladder got away from me. FWING! It flopped onto the pavement, nearly putting a dent in the van, and causing Barry to leap back with an oath.

A stocky man with sandy hair and a mustache was standing nearby, and despite himself, he couldn't help but laugh at our antics. Then he looked at me, sheepishly, and I started laughing with him.

Curiosity got the best of him, and he walked over. "What is that, a ladder?"

"Yes, and that's the sail from a 33-foot sailboat," I said, explaining Barry's plan to put the load on top of the 8-foot tall van. The man had regained his composure but looked skeptical. I was skeptical, too.

"How do we get the ladder on top of the van without using the ladder?" I asked Barry.

"We lift one end and then walk it up," he said. As the sandy-haired man watched, Barry and I each went to one end of the ladder to test the weight. I grunted, barely able to lift my end. "No problem," said Barry, who was busy tying things to the ladder.

Still, the man hung around, watching. He chatted shyly with me, and I learned that he lived in a nearby house overlooking the freeway. He had worked at the battery plant in Winston-Salem for many years.

He'd never traveled far, but on this Sunday evening, he was returning from a car show a couple of hours from home. His hobby was fixing up old cars. When he described some of the cars he'd restored, I commented, "That sounds more like a passion than a hobby." He almost blushed.

Then Barry handed me a rope and said, "Marl that end around the sail and the rungs." The sandy-haired man looked impressed with Barry's sailing word, but I rolled my eyes. "Showoff," I muttered.

While I was helping Barry tie the bundle together, our curious friend wandered away. I heard a car start up and drive away, and I figured it was him.

But as we started to lift the heavy load, he magically reappeared. Suddenly, the load was much lighter as a third set of hands appeared in just the right place. In about 20 seconds, the tough part of the job was done.

"That was so easy!" I exclaimed to the man. "You must have had all the weight."

"No, I thought you did," he said.

"It wasn't me," said Barry. All three of us grinned at each other.

We shook his hand in thanks, then he wished us safe travels and went away, for good this time.

After he left, I understood why he'd hung around and chatted, even though he was so shy. He was afraid that we wouldn't be able to get the ladder on the roof by ourselves. He'd hung around the overlook for an extra 15 minutes as night fell, just to help us lift it.

If he had asked me outright whether he should stay to help us, I would have said no, we didn't need any help. He simply stayed, without asking, and I was tickled to have his company.

Through encounters like this, I've learned to accept help when it is genuinely offered, even at times when I don't think I need it. When I allow someone to help me, they feel good about themselves, and that's a subtle, valuable gift I give them in return.

CHAPTER 9

ALWAYS SAY YES...

This is absolutely the best piece of travel advice I've ever heard: "Always say yes, and always take all your stuff."

These words of wisdom come from my friend Dave, whose adventures have taken him all over the world, from Europe to Central America to China and beyond. What he meant was, when an opportunity comes up, don't hesitate to accept it. But be sure to take all your belongings with you, because if it's not a good experience, you'll be free to move on to something else. Besides, one good situation often leads to the next. So if you have all your belongings with you, you can pursue the next opportunity with abandon...and then be sure to take all your stuff along for *that* one.

A few years ago, my friend Tina and I discussed the possibility that we were doppelgangers. She started a list of all the things we had in common, including the fact that we have the same hair color and complexion and are only three days apart in age. To this, we added first boyfriends with the same name and the fact that our first cars were brown Volkswagen Rabbits. When Tina told me she was adopted, I secretly wished that she was my twin sister, separated at birth.

Then Tina discovered her birth mother, Shirley, in Spokane, Washington. Reluctantly, I gave up the idea that we were secret twins.

When I met Shirley, I realized that Tina had lucked into the coolest birth-mother on the planet. Shirley was someone *I* needed to adopt.

A year later, as I started driving across the country by myself, I got lonely in eastern Washington. I had only been on the road for one day.

I looked at the map and realized I was not very far from Spokane. Perhaps I could contact Shirley and take her out to lunch. I rummaged through my notebook, but I couldn't find Tina's work number, so I called her husband, Will, at home.

"Hi, Will! I'm outside Spokane, and I need Tina's work number."

"OK, let me get it for you," he said, sounding very sleepy for 11 am. I heard him call across the room, "Hey, Tina, what's your work number?"

"Will? What are you doing?" I asked.

"I'm asking Tina for her work number," he said.

"What's Tina doing at home, instead of at work?" I asked.

"She's taking a vacation day. We're going camping this weekend," he said.

"Well, if Tina is at home, then I don't want her work number," I said.

"OK," he said, maddeningly. He didn't get the hint.

"I. Need. To. Talk. To. Tina." I said, very slowly. Finally, he handed her the phone and went to make himself a much-needed cup of coffee.

Despite admitting to still being in her jammies, Tina was completely coherent and was able to give me Shirley's phone number. With some trepidation, I called Shirley, whom I'd only met once — and to my relief, she remembered me. "Would you be free for a cup of coffee or some lunch today?" I asked. "Sure!" she said, giving me directions to her house. "I'm still in my jammies, but I'll wash my face and be out on the front porch. You're only about 10 minutes away."

At 11 am, I wondered if I was the only person awake, alert, and dressed in the entire state of Washington.

I pulled up in front of Shirley's house, which I recognized from a photo on Tina's fridge. It was an elegant 1903 Craftsman with a front porch big enough for a pool table. I knew this because Shirley had somehow acquired a pool table and placed it on the front porch.

It was probably 11:15 when I arrived, and she made me welcome, inviting me into the kitchen for iced tea. Right away, she asked me where I was planning to stay, and I said I was going to continue on the road and find a place later that night. "I have a guest room, and you're welcome to stay here," she offered. After sleeping in a tent by the side of US Route 2, it sounded heavenly, but I felt terrible about dropping in on such short notice.

"It sounds lovely, but I'd better keep moving," I said.

This was before I'd learned Dave's advice about "always say yes."

It was also before I learned about accepting help when it's offered.

Our conversation went from 0 to 60 mph, and it just kept going and going at that speed. We had talked for a couple of hours, non-stop, when she offered the guest room again.

"Are you sure you can't spend the night here?"

"Oh, no, I really should keep going," I said. I wanted to pinch myself, I felt so lucky. Only a few hours earlier, I'd been plunged into the depths of loneliness and boredom. Now here I was, talking with one of the most interesting artists I'd ever met. But I knew that although Shirley was retired, she had many friends and commitments

Shirley and Penny

I was grateful for the axe-murderer's escape.

and was busy with creative projects. I didn't want to get in the way; I'd just stopped for coffee.

Shirley told me she knew a wonderful place to have lunch, if I was willing to drive. She didn't have a working car; her little hatchback had stopped running after 21 years. Although her mechanic told her it was B.E.R. (Beyond Economic Repair), she wasn't ready to replace it, because it had been her mother's. She cheerfully lived without a car for a couple of months, walking and catching rides with her many friends.

"My kids think I'm nuts," she said.

We rolled down the hill in my tiny Geo Tracker to have lunch at a beautiful diner called Frank's. It was a historic railroad dining car converted to a restaurant, and Shirley knew both the owner and the craftsman who'd done the intricate wood inlays. Despite the fact that it sat beside the railroad tracks, so that it rumbled and shook authentically whenever another train went by, it was actually delivered to Spokane by truck.

We were on a conversational roll, with hardly time to eat or breathe between topics, when Shirley asked me, "Did you hear about the crazy man at the State Fair?"

"You mean the hypnotist?" That was a fascinating story she'd told me an hour or two earlier.

Shirley shook her head and launched into something completely different. "There's a state hospital near here for the mentally ill. Yesterday, they took a group of criminally insane patients to the State Fair, and one of them escaped. He's a murderer who once decapitated someone, and they still haven't caught him."

"Are you serious?" I said. My fork stopped in mid-air. I couldn't tell if she was teasing me, since I had been so adamant about camping out in my little tent that night. Now I wondered whether my trip would be cut short by an encounter with a real, live axe-murderer.

Yes, she was serious. Then our waiter came by, and we digressed to chat with him about the diner's decor for a little while.

After the waiter left, Shirley said, "Are you sure you don't want to spend the night and go to a play with me?"

I knew she really meant it. "Well, it does sound like a lot of fun. Twist my arm!"

She reached across the table and gave my arm a tweak. We grinned at each other, looking forward to the play and more conversation.

It had taken the threat of an axe-murderer to get me to finally give in and say, "Yes!" To this day, I am grateful for that axe-murderer's escape.

Back at the house, as I pulled my overnight bag out of the car, Shirley asked me a strange question. "How do you feel about clowns?" I wondered if this had something to do with the evening's activity. Did I have to dress up as a clown to go to the play?

I admitted that I didn't have a lot of feelings one way or the other about clowns. It was a slight fib. When I was a child, I hated clowns. When she asked the question, though, I realized I hadn't thought about clowns much in the last 30 years.

"You're not afraid of them, are you?" she continued.

"How do you feel about clowns?"

Now I was really wondering. I'd heard of people who were clown-phobic, and my childhood clown hatred may have been the result of a phobia. I shrugged and said I didn't think so, but I was bewildered.

It all made sense when I saw the purple and lavender guest room decorated with Shirley's clown collection. There were over 100 clown statues and dolls, plus a number of clown paintings and a pair of gi-ant stuffed clown-head slippers. I was surprised by the sensitive and artistic renderings (except for the slippers, which were pure kitsch), and I could have spent days studying them. I was fascinated, and now I knew that I no longer hated clowns.

Shirley and I had so much to talk about, I almost didn't leave the next day, either. Finally, in the early afternoon, we'd worked our way out to the front porch with my luggage. We were still telling stories, and Shirley was still in her nightgown. Then she peered over my shoulder and asked, "What's that sign?" I looked out and saw it, too, a white sign on the corner, several houses down.

I braced myself for the reaction. "It says 'Yard Sale,'" I answered, knowing that Shirley's obsession with yard sales was even greater than my own.

"Oh! Goodbye, then!" Shirley said, laughing. "I have to get dressed!"

We shared one last hug, and I walked to my car. I had said, "Yes." Now it was time to take all my stuff and go on to my next adventure.

CHAPTER 10

...AND ALWAYS TAKE ALL YOUR STUFF

Twenty years before I met Shirley, I had learned about the other half of Dave's travel advice: "Always take all your stuff." During that strange week on Key West, Barry and I kept our stuff packed, so that we could simply drive away from the crazy, violent situation if we needed to. "Always take all your stuff" meant we were free to stay, but only as long as it remained fun.

"Whatever you're doing, stop it!"

It remained fun at the house on Angela Street for much longer than I anticipated.

In the beginning of the two-year adventure we had in our 20's, the one we called The Interlude, Barry and I decided to drive to Key West. I'm not sure why, whether it was the southernmost point in the continental USA or the Jimmy Buffet Margaritaville culture that lured us down there. It just seemed like the thing to do.

Once there, we looked at the campground and decided that $25 a night was highway robbery for two people in a tent. We figured we might as well splurge and stay in a cheap hotel for two nights. It was only $45 a night for a European-style room with a shared bathroom at Eden House. What the heck, as long as we were spending freely, we might as well take a snorkeling cruise, and eat in some restaurants, and rent a bicycle-built-for-two. It seemed like a fun, romantic way to see Key West.

We walked down Simonton Street to a bike rental place and asked about a tandem. The one they produced had seen better days. It was a big, heavy thing, and the steering was somewhat wobbly.

"You should let me be the one in front," I said to Barry. "I have a better sense of direction."

He agreed, reluctantly, and we climbed onto the bike.

From the moment we took off down the street, the bicycle was out of control. We caromed in and out of traffic, over the center line, practically hitting parked cars. I blamed the weaving and wobbling on Barry, despite the fact that I was the one who was supposed to be steering. I shrieked and screeched, shouting over my shoulder — and causing more wobbles — "Whatever you're doing, stop it!"

But all he was doing was pedaling. And when he stopped, so did the bike. Then I was the one who was supposed to balance it, and I couldn't keep it upright with both of us on it.

Eventually, we parked the now-hated bicycle in front of a Cuban restaurant and went inside for lunch. We glared at each other over the small table and argued about who was responsible for the bicycle problems. Finally, we decided to take the damned thing back. We'd meant to keep it all day, but we hoped they would give us the hourly rate if we gave it back to them early.

After dropping off the bike, we were so relieved that we looked like lovebirds as we strolled back to our hotel. We were feeling right with the world again as we passed a man trying to attach a sign to a lamppost with some twine. He looked like he needed three hands, so Barry stopped to offer assistance.

It was an interesting sign, with a Keith Haring-style drawing of a man on it and the words "Estate Sale." While Barry fussed with the twine, tying sailing knots and multi-part purchases, I started chatting with the man, who had long wavy hair tied in a loose ponytail. He introduced himself as James and said his sale was just down the block.

The three of us walked down to James's house, a charming two-story Key West conch house with a white picket fence. The front yard was full of furniture, lamps, and tables loaded with household goods. A black-and-white polka-dotted shower curtain was hung on the front of the gingerbread-trimmed porch. The shower curtain was adorned artistically with multi-colored flyswatters. Along the picket fence, a pink-and-green-and-yellow sign proclaimed "Moveing Sale."

Barry and I perused the tables but didn't find anything we could use. We'd already removed the entire back seat from our Honda Civic, it was so full. Space was at a premium.

James had flopped down onto an expensive-looking navy blue sofa in the middle of the yard. I asked him, "Do you have any sheets? I'm looking for a full- or queen-sized flat sheet, but I don't see any here." At Bahia Honda, we'd found our down sleeping bags miserably hot and had agreed that we should pick up a sheet or two from a thrift store.

"Let me go inside and look," said James. He went inside the house and came to the front door with a sheet. Behind him, a dark-haired woman argued with him, saying loudly, "No, not that one! It's part of a set." He went back inside and got another, and we could hear her loudly telling him that was part of a set, too. Finally, he came outside and said, "I'm

The pink-and-green-and-yellow sign on the picket fence.

sure we have one somewhere. Can you come back tomorrow, or give me a call?" He wrote his phone number on a slip of paper.

In those days before cell phones, it was easier and cheaper to drop by in person than to find a phone and call James. So we returned the following day. Although the sign was still posted on the fence, there weren't any goods in the front yard. Shyly, we knocked on the door.

James greeted us as friends and invited us inside. I looked around curiously. In true Conch-house style, we entered a long hallway that ran through the middle of the house, with doors on either side. He led us through the house into the kitchen, which was at the very back, overlooking a shady backyard. After seating us at the table, he asked, "Would you like something to drink?"

We accepted a couple of sodas.

"What a cool table! Where did you get it?" I asked. The dining room table was teal and black formica, with five irregular sides that seated seven people. James admitted that he'd designed and built it himself. Then I started noticing other intriguing objects around the room, like the yellow-and-black shelves above the stove. He admitted he'd built those, too.

"Do you want to see some others?" he asked.

"Sure!"

James took us upstairs, where everything was eclectic. A lamp was painted with cow spots, and an old rusty fender on the wall sported dried flowers and a boomerang-shaped antenna. He had a unique eye for shapes, and had made table legs and shelf brackets in all sorts of shapes, from angular to organic. Bumper stickers, seashells, and plastic bugs were juxtaposed with bird nests, fly swatters, and ceramic kitsch. I was awed by the sheer creativity.

We stayed upstairs, sitting on the upstairs deck and looking across Simonton Street at the police station.

"My friends think I'm crazy for wasting my time on this stuff," he said of his art.

A construction worker by trade, he'd been injured falling off a roof and had received a disability settlement. The money was running out, though, so he was having a yard sale to raise funds. At least, that's what he told us then.

We sat on the deck, talking about life and traveling and art and music late into the night. There was so much to talk about with this amazing man who'd lived and worked in New York, Colorado, and California. He was quick to laugh, sharing our quirky sense of humor, but there was a dark side to his life, too. He hinted that things were not very good with his girlfriend, that his other friends weren't trustworthy, that he was angry and frustrated about his living situation.

At some point, we admitted to James that we didn't want to leave Key West, but we couldn't afford to stay at the hotel any longer. He told us about a place on the next island where we could camp for free. Barry and I looked at each other, excited. We'd move up to the free camping place the next day and spend a few more days exploring Key West.

We had arrived at James's at 3 pm, and when we finally got up to leave, it was past 3 am. He walked us down to the front door, and then said, "Wait, you don't have your sheet." He went upstairs and rummaged around, returning with a wadded-up flowered sheet. He wouldn't take any money for it. I wondered if it was part of a set.

The following day, we packed up and drove to Big Coppitt Key, the next island to the north. Following James's directions, we turned off at the Circle K mini-mart and found the beach. To our dismay, there were large "No Camping" signs posted along most of the beach.

We drove slowly along the beach and finally found a spot with some nice sea grapes that didn't have a "No Camping" sign right in front of it. Deep down, we knew the whole place didn't permit camping, but it was such a lovely beach, we just wanted to stay.

"Let's put our hammocks up and sleep in them tonight, instead of putting up the tent. Then it won't look like we're camping," I said to Barry. He probably thought I was being silly, but he agreed.

I was swinging in my hammock, reading a book and listening to music on my headphones, while Barry walked on the beach. I noticed him chatting with a man carrying a camera, but didn't pay much attention until the two of them walked over to my hammock.

"Hi, I'm Bill," the man introduced himself. He was a freelance photographer, and he'd come to this beach looking for women to photograph for a calendar. He was disappointed that the beach was so deserted.

"Say, have you got a bathing suit?" he asked me.

"Me?" I couldn't believe that anyone would want to take my picture.

I rooted around for my faded one-piece, and ducking behind the car, I put it on.

"That's great!" he said.

We walked out onto the beach, and he took a bunch of pictures of me perched like a mermaid on a chunk of dead coral.

"You know, for the calendar, they really prefer topless shots. But if you're not comfortable with that, it's OK. You know, you could probably arrange your hair somehow…"

Blame it on sunstroke, or vanity, but I decided to go along with his topless request. I had plenty of hair to cover myself, I thought.

I hadn't counted on the wind. As soon as I carefully arranged my hair over my breasts, the wind blew it straight out away from me. Then it got wet, and clumped together into one big strand. I gave up on modesty.

At the end of the afternoon, Bill thanked me and Barry profusely. We gave him our address, so he could let me know if he got any worthwhile photos.

We never heard from him again. Maybe there's a topless photo of me in a 1994 calendar. Or maybe not. I'll never know.

That night, we put on extra layers of clothes, sprayed ourselves with Off! mosquito repellant and climbed into our hammocks to sleep. I laid there for a long time, listening to the sound of the surf and the chirping of insects. Then bright lights swept across the road; a car was approaching.

It was a patrolling policeman. With his headlights aimed at us, he stopped behind our car and got out. "Uh oh," I thought, sitting up in my hammock.

"There's no camping here," he said.

"Oh, we aren't camping. We're just waiting to get some good sunrise pictures," I replied, lamely. He didn't crack a smile.

"You'll have to leave," he said.

The policeman waited while we untied our hammocks and got into our car, then he followed us out to the mini-mart on the highway. We pulled in, and he drove off down the highway. We sat under a bright buzzing sodium light in front of the Circle K, trying to figure out where to go.

"This camping spot was James's suggestion. Maybe if we call and tell him we got kicked out, we can pitch our tent in his yard tonight," I said to Barry.

Swatting the mosquitoes at the outdoor pay phone, Barry dialed James's number and told him what happened. "Can we come camp in your yard for the night?" he asked.

James said to come back to his house. We didn't have to pitch our tent, we could stay in one of the bedrooms.

I couldn't believe our luck. He gave us one of the two downstairs bedrooms; one door opened to the front porch and the other opened to the inside hallway. There was a queen-sized bed and a 70's-style mushroom lamp. James later put the lamp out in his yard sale, but when someone wanted to buy it, he couldn't part with it and put it back in our room.

It was still early, so we sat with James and Pam watching TV for a while. The two of them squabbled constantly. At some point, James asked if he could borrow $20 from us.

"No problem," I said, fishing a bill out of my wallet.

I doubted that I would ever see my $20 again. That was OK. I was still money ahead, given that we had a nice place to stay for the night. It was a lot less than the $25 campsites and $45 hotel rooms we'd found on Key West.

Pam took the money and left on an errand. Barry and I were tired, so we went to bed before she came back.

In the morning, James and Pam's squabbling escalated. We woke to the sound of the two of them in the room above us, screaming horrible things to each other at the top of their lungs. Still screaming

 obscenities, Pam stomped down the stairs and slammed the front door hard enough to shake our mushroom lamp.

That morning, I quietly packed our things, afraid that our presence might set off another storm when we saw James. We tiptoed out to the kitchen, but he was cheerful and showed no sign of the viciousness we'd overheard.

I thanked him for his hospitality, but he interrupted me. "You can't leave yet. I owe you twenty dollars." I looked at Barry, and he looked at me. James seemed like he genuinely wanted us to stay another night. "All right," we said.

We spent most of that day at South Beach, and when we returned in the afternoon, James handed me a twenty dollar bill. "Thanks!" he said, brightly.

In the evening, he came down to our room. "Hey, could I borrow $20 again?"

"Sure," I said, chuckling. I handed him the same twenty-dollar bill he'd given back to me earlier. Thus began an entire week where we remained packed, but we never left.

It was a few days before I understood what was going on: James and Pam were addicted to crack cocaine. In the evening, when the addiction was strongest, James would borrow $20 from us, and Pam would use it to go out and buy crack. They would take turns smoking it and enjoying the high. But in the morning, they were in withdrawal, which explained the screaming fights.

During the day, Pam had a part-time job renting scooters. When she returned from work, she was able to repay us $20 from her tip money. Then, in the evening, the addiction would take over and the two of them would need the money again.

The other problem with the house on Angela Street was the lack of water. The only bill James paid was the phone bill, because he considered his phone a necessity. He was months behind on his rent and his water

James couldn't part with the mushroom lamp
and put it back in our room.

bill, so the water had been turned off. That meant no showers, but at night, James would sneak over to the house next door, where the landlord lived, and fill buckets of water to flush the toilet.

As a host, he was embarrassed that he couldn't provide us with showers. He took it as a personal challenge to send us to the best — and most interesting — places to shower on Key West.

On our second day, he sent us to a motel called the Atlantic Shores. The motel itself wasn't remarkable, but the beach bar tucked behind it was a real eye-opener for a naive midwestern girl.

Both men and women were wearing thong bathing suits, which I had never seen, and which were outlawed on many beaches at that time. Some of the women were topless, including one woman with pierced nipples who was playing volleyball in the pool with the men.

Later, at the bar, I ended up next to her. Nonchalantly, as if I routinely conversed with topless women with pierced nipples (this was long before I ever went to Burning Man, where such things are commonplace), I asked how the game went. "The guys get a little rough, but I'm getting in shape this summer so I can keep up," she said, sipping her beer.

Barry and I swam in the pool and the ocean, drank a couple of margaritas, and at the end of the afternoon, took a long shower.

When we got back to James's house, he asked us about our showers. And he gave us back the twenty-dollar bill.

On Thursday, James decided to resume the yard sale. We helped him move the furniture out to the front yard, setting it up like an outdoor living room, with two sofas and one of his elegant original coffee tables between them.

The three of us sat on the shady porch for hours, chatting and playing Scrabble. Based on the fact that his yard sale sign was misspelled, I'd made the mistake of thinking James would be a bad speller. I was wrong. He beat both me and Barry by many points.

The next day, another twenty-dollar bill. And another shower location. This time, Pam gave us directions to her house.

We were puzzled. She seemed to live at James's house, but evidently, she had a husband and two children and a house across town.

"He'll be at work, and the kids will be at school," she told us, giving us the key.

That was probably the strangest shower of my life. Imagine going into someone's house, someone you don't even know, going upstairs to find the bathroom, removing your clothing, and taking a shower.

To make it even more surreal, there was a large plastic elephant in the shower — and the water sprayed out of the end of his trunk!

I was terrified that Pam's husband would come home unexpectedly and find two wet, naked strangers in the shower, cavorting with the children's shower elephant.

Meanwhile, we kept meeting other interesting people at James's house on Angela Street. One night,

Two wet, naked, strangers, cavorting with the children's shower elephant.

James was hanging out with a
tall, skinny fellow named Terry.
James had kicked Pam out of
the house, and the phone rang
over and over, at least 50 times.
He kept picking it up and hanging up on her.

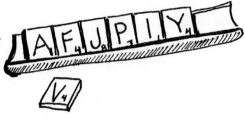

Terry was very reticent.

He beat us by many points.

When he left to "go get something," James told us a little
more about him. "He rips off the fags," he said. "He'll make friends
with one of them from out of town, and he'll say he knows where to
get some "stuff." Then they'll give him $20, and he'll take it and never
return." James laughed. "He did it to me once. I call him Twenty-
Buck Terry."

Terry eventually came back with "something," and he and James
took turns smoking crack and getting high. They never referred to it
by name. James would say he had a "hankerin'." He had a little closet
under the eaves, just tall enough to crawl into, that he called the
Hanker Inn. It was decorated with a collage of magazine clippings
and postcards and lit by an elegant chandelier. There was a buzzer in
the closet that was wired to the doorbell, because James was paranoid
about the police. He wasn't shy about smoking in front of me and
Barry, but Pam always crawled into the Hanker Inn to get high away
from us.

Barry and I had no interest in the drugs or alcohol that James and
his friends used. Neither of us had even seen crack cocaine before.
It was called a "rock," which was exactly what it looked like. "That
doesn't even look like something you could smoke," I told James. "If
you dropped that little chunk in the gravel driveway, how would you
find it again? You wouldn't be able to tell it from the other rocks."

He laughed at my naiveté and clutched his precious drug tightly
in his hand. "Oh, believe me, I would be able to tell which one it
was!"

James wasn't stupid; he knew very well how evil crack was. He
wished that he could get away from the drug and the friends who
used it, but the addiction was too strong for him.

Later that night, Terry said he was going to the Circle K for some beer. Barry gave him a dollar to get us some drinking water, and he never came back. We changed his nickname to "One-Buck Terry."

Another evening, we were in our room on the ground floor, laughing about something with James. A man walked in the main door, carrying a bottle of liquor. "Can I join you?" he asked. Barry and I looked at James, assuming that he knew the man.

"Do I know you?" James asked. "I don't think so, and you're in my house. Get out!"

The man went back into the hallway, but we didn't hear him leave. James followed him, and again we heard him demand that the man leave. Finally, we heard the front door slam shut.

James came back, shaking his head. "He was knocking on Samuel's door." Samuel slept in the room across the hall from me and Barry, but he was rarely there.

We went back upstairs, and from the upstairs deck, I saw the man with the bottle lurch out to the street corner, where another man was waiting. "Where'd ya go? I was waiting for you."

The two men started punching each other. Suddenly, they were literally rolling in Simonton Street, fighting and screaming obscenities at each other.

The fight didn't last long. I watched, laughing silently, as several policemen separated them and led them away in handcuffs. The men were oblivious to the fact that they were fighting directly in front of the police station!

Then again, the police seemed completely oblivious to the illegal activities in the house across the street.

Samuel was another interesting character that James had collected. "I met him sitting on the steps of a church one day," said James. "I just started telling him about all this shit and what's been happening. He's a real good listener."

My impression of Samuel was of a small man who smiled a lot but didn't speak English, which might explain why he was such a good listener. He slept at James' house, but I doubted that he paid rent. He was an illegal immigrant, a kind-hearted, hard-working man with three low-paying jobs and no car or bicycle. He spent all his time working and sleeping and sent his money home to elderly parents in Mexico.

I wondered what Samuel thought about the screaming fights and lack of water in the house. Maybe he thought that was normal American behavior, part of our culture.

We spent over a week in James' house, a week in which Barry and I always intended to leave the next day. One morning, I realized that we had landed in Margaritaville, the kind of place where time goes more and more slowly and nobody gets anything done. It was time to "take all our stuff," which had never been unpacked anyway, and drive back north.

I said, firmly, "James, we really have to leave today."

He was terribly disappointed and insisted on giving us very detailed directions to the scooter shop before we could leave. "You have to stop and say goodbye to Pam," he said.

Barry and I looked at each other, afraid of yet another delay.

Then James added, by way of explanation, "She has your twenty dollars."

CHAPTER 11

WRITING MY PLANS IN THE SAND

After a chance encounter with a stranger like James, I sometimes have to throw out my plans completely. Some idea, some suggestion from them takes hold, and I recognize that it's a lot better than what I originally was going to do.

Barry and I were camping in Collier-Seminole state park in Florida when we heard about a canoe trail through the Everglades. It was an easy two-day trip through the mangroves, well-marked with navigation aids on pilings. Halfway along the route was a remote campsite on an island, inaccessible to cars, where we could pitch our tent.

At the time, we not only had all our belongings and camping gear in our Honda Civic, we had a very large aluminum canoe tied on top. All we had to do was untie the canoe, fill it with our camping gear, and follow the red and green markers.

That canoe was so large, it could hold most of the stuff we had in the tiny car. This included our tent, double sleeping bag, pillows, two-burner stove, dishes, dishpan, cooking pots, food, 48-quart cooler, and several changes of clothing. We even tossed a couple of folding chairs on top. The only thing we left in the car was the teddy bear.

We didn't see anyone else on the water all day. As we paddled along the twisting waterway that cut through the dense mangroves, I began envisioning a romantic campsite with a cheery fire. We'd be alone together, two lovebirds, miles from civilization, with no one to bother us.

Soon, he had a tiny blaze.

"Oh!" I exclaimed, disappointed. We had come around a bend and could see the island where we'd be camping. It was very tiny, and there was a small, strange-looking craft pulled up on the minuscule beach.

So much for our private, romantic getaway. On the only island for miles with space to camp, there was a small green tent.

We beached our canoe and unloaded our piles of gear in a swarm of mosquitoes. Barry found a level, sandy place to set up our tent, barely a hundred feet from the other one. I created a camping kitchen next to the remains of a prior occupant's campfire, arranging our cooler, stove, and chairs. We were rummaging in our boxes and bins for ingredients to cook dinner when our neighbor crawled out of his tent, slapping at the ferocious biting insects.

"Hi!" he said, yawning. Evidently, he'd been napping. He rummaged around in his tent, and then came over, holding a can of chili in his hand. We introduced ourselves; his name was Doug.

The conversation was a little awkward, in part because of the forced proximity, and partly because we were all slapping and dancing frantically because of the mosquitoes. "I'm going to make a fire; the smoke should drive them away," said Doug.

As Barry and I watched, Doug removed the wrapper from his can. He arranged some leaves and twigs on top of it and then lit the small piece of paper with a single match. Soon, he had a tiny blaze, and he carefully added more twigs and sticks and larger pieces, creating a cheery campfire without any of the tools or piles of newspaper we were accustomed to using.

Then he opened the can with his Swiss Army knife and set it in the fire to heat.

I was impressed and completely embarrassed. All he needed to cook and eat his dinner and to keep the mosquitoes at bay were the can, one match, and the Swiss Army knife.

In my boxes and bags, I had a Swiss Army knife, too. However, I never used it — I carried it in addition to a paring knife, a filleting knife, a full set of silverware for four people and a large can opener. I also had a full complement of skillets and saucepans, pot holders, two sizes of plates, glasses, mugs, and bowls. I had three varieties of mosquito repellents. I had a hatchet and a saw, some newspaper, and a handful of lighters, as well as matches. I felt foolish for bringing it all. Our canoe would have been so much lighter and easier to paddle if we'd packed like Doug.

Even though Doug was in his mid-20's, the same age as Barry and I were at the time, we had a lot to learn from him about resourcefulness and traveling light. We spent the entire evening sitting around that cheery fire, listening to his stories and asking him questions.

I'll never regret the change in agenda that night, missing out on my romantic evening with Barry. We have made up for our lost romantic evening many times since then — but hearing Doug's stories was a once-in-a-lifetime experience.

After he graduated from college, Doug, who was from New York City, had taken advantage of a program that allowed young people from other countries to live and work in Australia. It was the first we'd heard of it, and he told us it was fairly restrictive. "You can't stay for very long, and you can't take any of the good jobs away from the Australians," he said. He'd held dozens of menial jobs in the year he was there — dishwashing, garbage collecting, lawn-mowing. Whenever he quit a job or got fired, he'd quickly take the least-desirable job on the planet: A telemarketer. In those days, before cell phones, pay phones were his biggest expense, and a telemarketing job gave him access to a phone to find his next job.

The most interesting job he had that year was also the worst. He'd heard about a position as a roustabout for a circus. It sounded like fun to run away with the circus, hanging out with lion-tamers and trapeze artists. But once he got into it, he was dismayed. The clowns and the dwarves, and especially the management, treated him terribly. Behind the scenes, the circus world was a dark and evil one where people played by cruel, dangerous rules. He left without getting his last paycheck.

As the Polish proverb says, "Not my circus. Not my monkey."

Doug finally ran afoul of the authorities, because he was having so much fun that he continued working low-wage, undesirable jobs after his work permit expired. Eventually, he got kicked out of Australia, so he trekked through southeast Asia with a backpack before returning to his parents' home in New York City.

When we met him, he'd had a few years of living and working in New York at a nine-to-five job, but it didn't suit him very well, so he quit. He was traveling around in a small hatchback, like ours, with his folding kayak and his camping gear, figuring out what to do next. He was free to go anywhere, except for Australia.

At that time, Barry and I had left our nine-to-five jobs in Washington D.C. and were traveling with our canoe and our camping gear, trying to figure out what to do next. We were free to go anywhere, including Australia. My biggest regret, to this day, is that we didn't.

We did learn a lesson from Doug. Twenty years later, we listened to a couple of strangers, and we did change our plans.

That was how I discovered my secret super-power, the power to repel bears with just my voice.

We'd left our friends' sailboat, *Complexity*, that morning in Juneau, Alaska. Our trip to Skagway aboard an Alaska State Ferry took all day, and the sunshine was warm and the views were breathtaking. After the ship docked, all of the other passengers departed by car. We trailed behind them, crossing the parking lot on foot and carrying our belongings in two borrowed frame backpacks. It was the first time we'd traveled this way, with all of our belongings on our backs instead of carried by car, canoe, or bicycle.

Walking the few blocks to the campground, my shoulders and back reminded me that I was not a backpacker.

It was in Skagway that Barry and I had to make a decision. We had come from Seattle by water, and I wanted to retrace the route of the 1897 Klondike gold miners. But could I hike over Chilkoot Pass with this backpack?

If not, we could take the scenic White Pass & Yukon Railroad over the pass. Either way, we would then catch a bus from Whitehorse to Dawson City, the site of the Yukon Gold Rush.

The campground in Skagway catered mostly to RVs, but there was a small tenting area. It was just a patch of grass with a few trees and a single picnic table. One tent was already set up there, and I hoped its occupants would be willing to share the table with us.

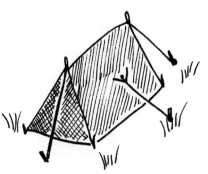

I hoped its occupants would be willing to share the table with us.

A short time later, after we'd set up camp, the neighbors returned, two older gentlemen who said hello in accented English. They politely said they were very willing to share the picnic table with us.

Mannfred, the older of the two, was a trim silver-haired man in his 70's. He was outgoing and wanted to talk, but he spoke almost no English. His companion, Peter, spoke more English, but was soft-spoken and too busy with their gear to serve as interpreter.

So, with Mannfred, Barry and I used a mixture of English, German, sign-language, and pictures to communicate. It took a while to get the story, but it was worth every minute.

Living in East Germany, Mannfred spent his entire life wishing he could see the world, but he didn't have the freedom to do so. "I could go to Poland or Russia — bah!" He made a face at the vacation choices he was allowed in those days. Then, when the Berlin Wall fell in 1989, he suddenly found that he had both the freedom and the money to achieve his dreams.

Mannfred made a bucket list of the places he wanted to see in his life — places like Australia, the United States, South America, China. He had specific goals; he not only wanted to see Africa, he wanted to climb Mount Kilamanjaro. It took him two tries, but he eventually achieved that goal.

Another very specific goal eluded him for even longer. Mannfred wanted to paddle the mighty Yukon River, but he needed a guide, and he didn't know where to find a German-speaking one. Finally, using the Internet, he found what he needed: Someone who had

paddled the Yukon river every summer for 30 years, who spoke flu-
ent German, and, to his amazement, lived a few miles away in West
Berlin. He'd found Peter.

Peter joined us at the table for a little while. His English was
much better than Mannfred's, so he was able to tell his story a lot
more quickly.

Peter was only a little younger than Mannfred. He'd grown up in
West Germany, free to travel anywhere he wanted during his lengthy
summer vacations. Instead of seeing the entire world, he specialized
in one place, the Yukon. Every summer, he flew to Canada and explored his favorite river.

The two of them spoke at length about the paddling trip they'd
just completed, from Whitehorse to Dawson City.

"Did you see many bears?" I asked.

"Oh, yes," said Mannfred, "many, many bears." He seemed
pleased to have seen so much wildlife. Peter said the bears were on
the banks, eating berries, while he and Mannfred were safely in a
canoe out in the wide river.

I looked at Barry. I was scared of bears, worried about backpack-
ing in a region full of them. Since we were more comfortable on the
water than with backpacks, maybe we could rent a canoe and paddle
the Yukon River, instead of facing the grizzlies on foot!

After months of wanting to retrace the route of the Yukon gold
rush on foot, I suddenly changed my mind. Now, I wanted to retrace
the water portion of the route, because I thought there would be
fewer bears swimming around in the river. Thank goodness we had
met Peter and Mannfred in the campground; the information they'd
given us about canoeing had probably saved our lives.

Peter gave us the number of the canoe outfitter in Whitehorse,
and with one brief phone call from the campground pay phone, our
new plans were made. We would take the White Pass and Yukon
Railroad up to the pass, catch a bus to Whitehorse, and then pick up
the canoe and the groceries we needed to paddle the river.

The outfitter rented us a canoe, paddles, life jackets, and something called "Bear Barrels" for our food. These were a couple of plastic
bear-proof containers, cylindrical, with elaborate fasteners, and very
well-sealed. Barry said that if a bear did get his paws on one, he'd just

dribble the indestructible thing like a basketball, unable to get a grip on it.

We didn't have many choices for provisioning in Whitehorse, just a couple of liquor stores and a giant Wal-Mart with a parking lot full of American RVs. Although we walked all over town looking, there was one item on our list that neither Wal-Mart nor any other store carried: An air horn. In other words, a super-loud scare-the-bears horn. We finally set out without one.

During the next nine days on the river, Barry and I were utterly alone in the wilderness. We saw only three or four people in other boats, never closer than a mile away. It was just what I had wished for, that earlier time in the Everglades. Every night, we were alone together, two lovebirds, miles from civilization, with no one to bother us.

During the day, we paddled lazily in the four-to-five knot current. At night, though, we beached the canoe to cook our meals and set up our tent.

I hadn't stopped to realize that we would be sleeping on shore with the bears, unprotected.

Obviously, we survived.

On our last night, before climbing into my sleeping bag, I headed into the woods to go to the biffy. Although it was past midnight, we were so close to the Arctic Circle that it wasn't dark, just a very deep twilight. I walked away from our cheery campfire, singing my new favorite song by the Arrogant Worms at the top of my lungs — "Canada's Really Big."

Singing was something I'd been doing throughout the trip, although I cannot carry a tune in a bucket. Whenever we beached the canoe, I was the first one to clamber out, and I did not want to be a bear snack.

I figured the safest thing was to let any bears in the vicinity know that I was there, and since I didn't have an air horn,

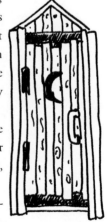

Yukon Biffy

"Just my voice... But it's working!"

there was only one way to do so. I had to make a lot of noise myself.

So I introduced myself to them. I called "HELLOOOOOOO," loudly, into the woods where I presumed many bears were hanging out, listening to me. I made impassioned speeches to them. I stomped my feet and rattled the bushes. I thumped my paddle against the canoe.

Mostly, though, I sang silly songs to the unseen bears.

I say unseen, because despite what Peter and Mannfred told us, we never saw a single bear. On that last night, however, I found out that they were still in the neighborhood.

On my way back from the biffy, singing the third verse at one o'clock in the morning, I heard a crashing in the underbrush. My heart stopped. Had my singing finally offended a large, angry grizzly bear, who was charging out of the underbrush to make the horrible noise go away?

Instead, across a small creek, a man appeared. He was the first human being I'd seen besides my husband for over a week, and I just stared. And stopped singing.

"Hi!" said the man.

"Hi," I said, in a very small voice. "I thought you might be a bear," I admitted, which made him laugh. I went on to tell him that for our entire trip down the river, I'd been singing and talking loudly to keep the bears away.

"Oh, bears are nothing, as long as you have something to keep them away." He showed me his whistle, on a lanyard around his neck, and the mace spray he carried in a holster on his belt. "So what have you got, eh? For the bears?"

I thought to myself, this Canadian was a little dense. Hadn't I just told him?

"Just my voice…but it's working! We haven't seen a single bear."

It was his turn to stare in shocked silence. "Wow," he said, shaking his head. "You're lucky." Then he told me about the many bears he'd seen in the past few days, along the same stretch of the river where Barry and I had been paddling.

When we said goodnight, the man went back to his campsite, armed with his bear spray and whistle. I returned to Barry and our tent, armed only with my powerful, bear-repelling singing voice.

"So, what have you got
for bears, eh?"

CHAPTER 12

THE BEST WAY TO TALK IS NOT TO

I feel pretty lucky, even honored, when a stranger comes up to me and initiates a conversation. I never know where the conversation is going to go, but I'm always interested in finding out. Oftentimes, it's just surface stuff: A friendly comment about the weather. A lighthearted quip about the music. A compliment on my jewelry or clothing.

Other times, though, that's just the beginning. We start at the surface and delve into some of our deepest, innermost thoughts. The fact that we are strangers and can simply walk away from each other provides a sort of safety net.

When someone approaches me, I draw them out through compassionate listening, I let them tell their stories without interruption. I remember that I have a choice: Is it more important to tell my story or to hear theirs?

Sociologist Charles Derber has coined the phrase "conversational narcissism," which is when people constantly try to turn the attention in a conversation towards themselves. If I'm talking with a friend, and they keep talking about themselves and don't stop and let me talk, I get frustrated. "Hey, what about me? What about *me?*" is my silent refrain.

It can be different when I meet a stranger. I want to learn about this mysterious person. Telling

His face lit up like a light bulb.

them about me is optional. I don't mind if they hang onto the conversational "ball," telling me everything that's on their mind.

I was up at the very northeast corner of Maine, in a small old town called Lubeck. The only pay phone was in front of the convenience store, which was a hopping place at 8:05 pm (the grocery store closed at 8:00 pm). Barry was using the pay phone for a long call with his mother, going over our mail and taking care of business. To entertain myself, I stood on the sidewalk in front of the convenience store and watched the people who came and went from the place.

A sedan pulled up with an older couple inside. As they were getting out, a little clumsily, because they were not very spry, the fellow looked on the ground and found something beside his car. His face lit up like a light bulb, it delighted him so much, and he slowly bent down and picked it up. "Guess people just don't like these ol' pennies any more," I heard him say to the woman as they went into the store.

On their way out, as the man walked past me, he smiled and said hello, inviting me into a conversation. I took that opportunity to ask him an interested question.

"What did you find in the parking lot that made you so happy?"

He responded with a twinkle in his eye, "Years ago, I promised God that any money I found would be His." I nodded, to let him know I was listening, and waited for more. Encouraged, he continued. "One time, I was down on my luck, and I found a twenty-dollar bill. It was real tempting to keep that for myself! But when you make a promise to the Lord like that, you better keep it!"

He continued talking for a little while about his lucky finds, and what he had done with them over the years. Then he winked at me, wished me safe travels, and drove into the night.

The Maine encounter illustrates the importance of asking an *interested* question, and then taking the time to give the other person my full attention while I listen to their answer.

There's a common not-interested question that we are all familiar with: "How are you?" To which a polite person is supposed to reply, "I'm fine," even if they are not.

But I like to turn "How are you?" into an interested question, so I have a chance to strike up conversations with strangers. I do this by using different emphasis. For example, I might ask, "How *are* you?" or "How are *you* today?"

Then there's this version: "How are you *doing?*"

Barry and I once stopped at a campground in Villa Nueva, New Mexico. We were hot, tired, and fractious as we walked around the nearly-empty campground, looking for a place to set up our tent. We were looking for privacy, so we disregarded the prettiest area along the river, where two sites were already occupied.

When we walked past those sites, a booming voice suddenly rang out, "How're you gals *doin?*"

At the time, Barry was clean-shaven and wore his hair in a style that today is called a mullet: Neatly cut on top, long in the back, but very evenly cut and brushed. So from a distance, we might have appeared as two girls. We stopped and looked at each other, then broke into unexpected giggles as we turned to see who had spoken.

The voice belonged to a tall, friendly-looking bearded guy carrying a musical instrument that I thought was a guitar (I later found out it was a dobro). He walked right up to us, stuck out his hand, and introduced himself, saying, "Hi, I'm Harley, and this here is Annabelle."

Annabelle had an acoustic guitar, and when she spoke, I realized it was her beautiful singing voice I'd been hearing across the campground. We were so charmed that after a bit of conversation, we decided to set up camp right next to their site. Our need for distance and privacy was forgotten, and our fractiousness had evaporated.

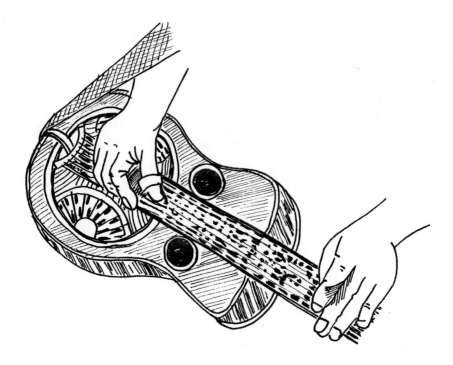

I later found out Harley was playing a dobro.

We had intended to stay for one night and hurry on towards Las Vegas. Instead, we lingered at Villa Nueva for several days, enjoying Harley and Annabelle's music, sharing meals around the campfire, listening to stories, and feeling like family.

I even crawled out of my tent at sunrise, bleary-eyed, just to take walks in the campground with Harley's mother, Winnie. After raising a family of boys, she and her husband had taken up a nomadic life, living out of suitcases as Harley Sr. moved from one engineering job to another across the USA. As a newcomer to the nomadic lifestyle, I found myself hanging on every word from this wise and matter-of-fact woman.

I was learning to listen.

We'd stopped at Villa Nueva for the scenery, but I learned from our new friends that encounters with people were more magical, more precious than scenery and history and wildlife. I recognized the

It was Annabelle's beautiful singing voice I'd been hearing.

importance of flexibility, of being willing to change plans when an opportunity to get to know a new person presented itself.

When we finally left the campground, with everyone waving goodbye, I felt sad and lonely. I didn't recognize that I was leaving with a new skill, a new ability to talk with strangers.

The following night, we set up camp in a primitive national forest campground. There were no facilities, not even a pit toilet, so we didn't expect to have neighbors. To my surprise, a small green car parked beside ours, and a man got out and set up a tent.

I was incredibly curious, because like us, he seemed to have everything he owned in the car. The campground was primitive, no run-

Ron had a good job, but he still had to live out of his car.

ning water or electricity, yet I could see a toaster and small television
in his back seat.

That night, at several thousand feet elevation, it became so cold
that the three of us had to share a campfire to stay warm, and the
man, whose name was Ron, had a chance to tell us the story of his
life. It was pure conversational narcissism — he started out sober and
became progressively more inebriated, and he didn't give us a chance
to say much more than "uh-huh" and "wow."

But Ron's words kept me on the edge of my seat.

He was a nomad, too, of a different kind. His tent was his home,
and he stayed in a state park for two weeks at a time. When he reached
the 14-day stay limit, he would move to the national forest for a few
days, until the rules permitted him to return to the state park for another 14 days. He preferred the state parks, because with electricity,
he could enjoy his TV and his toaster!

At one time, he'd been a forester, until he fell out of a tree and suffered life-threatening injuries. Stuck in a hospital and rehabilitation
center for months, he looked around and decided to take up a new

career in healthcare. Now he worked for a nursing agency, making a very good salary as a contract nurse-anesthetist.

It sounded like a good move, to put the past behind him and find a new career. Yet it was apparent that something in his past was holding him back, so that he still had to live out of his car. I sat at the campfire for hours, listening, trying to understand what it was.

He complained that rents in the Santa Fe area were too high, that everyone wanted to rent to tourists, so he couldn't afford an apartment. He'd left belongings all over the country in U-Store units, but more than once, he'd simply stopped paying the rent and abandoned his belongings. Hearing him talk about walking away from several marriages with children, watching him drink heavily, I could see why someone with a good job, highly skilled, well-paid, and in demand, might still have trouble settling down and affording an apartment. He had a monkey on his back.

I was genuinely interested in Ron's complex hard-luck story. I was just as interested in the stories I heard from Winnie and Harley and the anonymous man in Maine. Listening is a beautiful gift that I can give to any person, whether they are a stranger or not.

*It didn't matter that I only understood
one word out of ten.*

I don't even have to speak the same language to give and receive this gift.

In a tiny village in Portugal, Barry and I went looking for a restaurant. We found a place in an ancient stone building with a chalkboard out front that had a sort of rough menu written on it. When we went

*We were hungry
and trusting.*

inside, there were tables and lamps, but we were the only customers. A plump, motherly woman who wore an apron and had her sleeves rolled up came out from the kitchen to take our order; evidently, she was the cook, waitress, and dishwasher. Our slow, limited Portuguese was no match for her rapid-fire speech, and she spoke no English. We managed to convey the message that we were hungry and trusting, and that she could bring us whatever she wanted to cook.

She brought us some excellent wine, soup, and bread. The main dish was a rich, creamy casserole that had us practically licking our plates. Afterwards, she insisted on bringing us a desert course of cheese with jam on it, even though we pantomimed that we were stuffed.

The main dish was so incredible, I desperately wanted to figure out what was in it. So, with the help of my dictionary, I asked her, even though I wasn't sure how I'd understand the answer.

To my surprise, she invited us back into the restaurant's kitchen, where she showed us all the components of the casserole. It included bacalháo, or salt cod; potatoes; onions; a rich white cheese sauce; and a crunchy crumb topping. She demonstrated how she had assembled it, and even pointed to the marking on the oven showing the temperature at which she'd baked it. She was so proud, and so willing to share what she knew about cooking this native Portuguese dish, that it didn't matter that I only understood one word out of ten. I simply basked in that warm, friendly kitchen as I listened and observed.

To listen, or not-talk, is a wonderful way to get to know people, even when I don't understand a word they say.

CHAPTER 13

TAMING CHIPMUNKS

I know what it takes to get a chipmunk to take a peanut from my hand — I have to be quiet, and I have to hang around for a while. Human beings who are strangers can be just like cute wild chipmunks, poking their heads out of their hidey-holes to check me out. They're not really unfriendly, just suspicious of the unknown and not used to me.

When I come to a new place, I try to hang around for a few minutes, hours, or days. After I let a little time pass, I'll start to see the people and the place differently; I'll start to see some patterns. After the local people have seen me a few times, they are more likely to open up and talk.

Getting candy from strangers is like giving peanuts to wildlife. The passage of time makes it easier for both sides to set aside our initial fear and negative judgments.

Many, many times, I have initially had a negative reaction to someone who later became a friend. It has happened so often that now, when I find myself making a snap negative judgment about a stranger, I deliberately take a deep breath and think, "This person could be your new best friend by the end of the week."

Reedville, Virginia is a pretty little town on Chesapeake Bay that was named for Elijah Reed, who opened a fish-processing plant there in the 1800's. When we sailed there once, I learned that there were two classes of people who lived there: "Been Heres" and "Come Heres." In other words, people with roots in Reedville, and those who had recently purchased property there.

How do they define "recently?"

Barry and I were walking around Reedville when I noticed a bumper sticker. "Look at that," I said, poking him with my elbow. It said, "Elijah Reed was a Come Here."

There are plenty of people who accept this sort of thinking, and it can prevent them from talking with strangers. Me, I don't mind being a newcomer. I'm always interested in other people's lives, even if they have never gone anywhere. If I communicate that, they will often open up. Sometimes, they're even interested in my new and fresh perspective.

I can't say that I had any memorable encounters in Reedville, maybe because I was a "Come Here." More likely, though I didn't spend enough time in the town. My experience in Summit, South Dakota was completely different. I spent enough time there.

There are places on this earth where strangers simply do not go. Without tourism or foreign commerce, the people who live their day-to-day lives in those places become the most shy critters of all. The million-dollar question is, how long does it take for a visitor to those places to stop being a stranger?

The sign that changed the course of my trip.

I'd spent a few days crossing South Dakota on a series of two-lane roads, and frankly, it was mind-numbingly boring. One gray, drizzly morning, the highlight of my life was simply crossing Interstate 29. As I crossed the overpass, I considered taking the on-ramp and jumping into the river of cars going Someplace Else.

Luckily, I didn't. One mile later, I saw two signs in a cornfield that changed the course of my trip.

One said, "Summit, population 267." The other said, "High Plains Cafe." An arrow on the cafe sign pointed across the cornfields.

I turned right, between two cornfields, crossed a set of railroad tracks, and came into Summit. The town itself wasn't much to look at, but there were lots of cars angle-parked outside the High Plains Cafe. Evidently, the food was good, or the locals did not have discriminating taste.

I crossed the street in the pouring rain, walked into the cafe, and stopped in the tiny vestibule. Fourteen pairs of men's eyes stared at me. Thirteen baseball caps. Conversation stopped. I stood, frozen, clutching my notebook.

I waited for the waitress to meet my eyes, but she was deliberately ignoring me. I say this because she was standing three feet away from me, talking to the four men closest to the door. "It's raining," she complained to them, enunciating the words as if talking to children. She sighed, loudly. "So it gets really busy in here." Evidently, the additional bother wasn't worth the additional tips.

I guess I represented additional bother. When she was done taking their order, she walked away without even looking at me.

The door opened, and a man came into the vestibule. Another waitress came over, and she ignored me even more blatantly, talking to the man behind me, and then walking away. How long should I stand my ground? Was getting served here a matter of principle?

Finally, waitress number two came back. "Can I help you?" She looked like she didn't want to.

"I'd like to order some food" I said. She stared at me, suspiciously.

It's the notebook, I thought. I always carry it into restaurants, so that I can review my notes at meals. But she probably thought I was selling something, or maybe a health inspector.

Finally, she shrugged. "OK."

"Can I sit?" I asked.

"Sure."

"Anywhere?"

"Yeah," she answered, maddeningly walking away again.

I sat in a booth by the window and took in my surroundings. Conversation had resumed, and an older couple had come in with two toddlers, so I wasn't the only female customer any more. Now there were fifteen baseball caps, since one of the toddlers wore one.

Counting the calendars on the walls, I became downright hopeful. William Least Heat-Moon always said the quality of a cafe could be measured by the number of calendars on the walls. This one was a real four-calendar cafe. One of the four hung beneath a sign that said, "Try our new deep-fried Twinkies."

Sadly, the food was not up to the calendar rating. Four triangles of burnt white toast perched atop two overcooked eggs and some greasy sausage. The coffee was good, but there was no cream or milk, just packets of powdered coffee whitener and pink saccharine next to the cafe-issue sugar dispenser and salt and pepper shakers.

After my coffee cup and my water glass had been empty for about 10 minutes, the waitress remembered me. Either she felt badly about the way she'd treated me, or she recognized that her tip was getting close to the penny level, because she said, "Sometimes we tend to forget people when we get all these regulars." She nodded her head to the table against the wall, where four men were playing cards and talking loudly.

After she walked away, I found myself wondering, what would happen if I came in every day for a week?

That thought took hold. For almost an hour, I watched people come and go from the place, and none of them received the reception I had. They all knew each other, and greeted each other accordingly. The four card-players attracted three others who sat down and watched the game. A young man came in with a beautiful blonde toddler, and she sat in Grandpa's lap while he played cards. Her father, across the room, chatted with some other men while incongruously holding a large stuffed koala bear.

The waitress never brought me a check; I was forgotten again. I went up to the cash register, and while I waited, I read a laminated newspaper clipping on the counter. It was a recent letter to the editor of the Watertown newspaper, about 30 miles up the road, sent by some travelers who'd stopped here for a meal. In it, they gushed praise about the High Plains Cafe and its friendly and generous attitude. How could they be writing about the same place?

A man who I hadn't seen before rang up my breakfast. If the waitresses registered "one" on the warmth-to-strangers scale, he was about a "four." Out of ten.

Sometimes, I am absolutely amazed at the things that come out of my mouth.

As I paid for my food, I heard myself asking, "Do you know of anyone who has a cabin or a room to rent around here?" It was as if I was possessed. What was I thinking?

His initial reaction was no, he didn't know anyone. Then he said, "You might try asking over at the bank, though. They have some folks who rent places."

left the diner and walked back to my car. The rain had lessened, and as I was about to unlock the driver's door, I noticed where I was parked. I was right in front of the door of the bank.

I put the key back in my pocket as my feet — they seemed to have a will of their own — carried me into the bank. On the wall in the entry was a piece of paper listing some places for rent and their phone numbers. I walked up to the teller, a middle-aged lady, and asked about them.

"The man at the cafe sent me over here. Do you know anything about a place I might rent for the week?" Like the man at the cafe, she initially shook her head, then she paused and said, "Wait a minute. There's a lady who works here who rents out an apartment across the street."

She walked over to a bank office, spoke to the woman inside, and gestured me over. I asked my question a third time, and this time, the answer was positive.

"I have a furnished apartment across the street; when would you be looking to stay?"

"Right now, I answered. "For about a week."

She looked quite surprised. "It's only available until the festival this weekend." I looked at her calendar and realized that was six nights. Like a woman who was still possessed, I said I'd take it.

The woman, whose name was Tina, told me to wait at the bank while she went over to see if it was ready. While she was gone, I chatted with another bank employee, a motherly-looking woman. All of the people working in the bank were women, and this one mentioned a bank vice president, also a woman.

It seemed like the women did most of the work in Summit, and the men hung out at the cafe, drinking coffee and playing cards.

As tactfully as possible, I mentioned my experience as a stranger at the cafe. "I wondered to myself, if I go back every day for a week, will I be a regular?"

She chuckled. "If you go back tomorrow, you'll be a regular."

"If I went back in there right now, would I be a regular?" I asked. She laughed out loud, "Yes, absolutely."

Tina came back and led me over to the apartment. The low building was brown and nondescript. We walked into a featureless hallway lit with harsh fluorescent bulbs, and she unlocked the door to apartment number one.

I caught a whiff of fresh paint and new carpet smell as we walked into the one-bedroom apartment. The living room was furnished with a big sofa and three immense armchairs, the kind that can swallow a whole person. There was a dining table with four straight-backed chairs.

I paid her in cash. "If you need anything, we're in the red log house on the other side of the railroad tracks," she said.

I spent most of the rainy day in the apartment, writing. When there was a break in the clouds, I walked to the tiny grocery store for teabags and milk. There wasn't much real food in the store, just some dusty cans and a lot of chips and beer. The cashier was on the phone; she took my money but otherwise ignored me. Just like the cafe. Why had I decided to stay here?

As evening fell, with hardly any food in the apartment, I started thinking about the bar and grill next door. The cafe was only open for breakfast and lunch, but the motherly woman at the bank had told me I could get dinner at the bar. She said it was the kind of place a girl could go alone.

Still, I wished it wasn't Friday night. It would be nice to ease into a place like that gently, starting on a Tuesday afternoon. In my whole life, I had never gone into a bar alone.

After my experience with the cafe, I decided to go empty-handed, without my notebook. This time, I wasn't going to be mistaken for someone from the liquor board, or the health inspector's office.

It was still daylight when I walked into the entryway, and a couple of teenaged girls followed me in. I thought to myself, "This won't be so bad, if they're here."

But when I pushed open the smoked glass door, I was intimidated. It was a classic bar, dark and full of cigarette smoke, decorated with beer signs and posters. There were some people at tables, and one man at the bar. He looked me over when I walked in, his eyes traveling down, and up, and down again. I felt like fresh meat.

Luckily, the waitresses here were not like the ones at the cafe. They both smiled at me, although they gave their attention to the teenaged girls first. I finally asked, tentatively, "I can sit anywhere?" "Sure!"

All the tables seated at least four. I sat down at one on the far side of the room, wanting my back against a wall. But the waitress who came over disarmed me completely with her friendliness. "Are you here by yourself?" she asked. When I nodded, she said, "You should sit at the bar, so we can talk."

I followed her back across the room to the bar. The man who'd looked me over had left, so I had my choice of stools. I felt awfully exposed, sitting at the bar in the middle of the room, but the waitress, whose name was Lynn, was so friendly that I didn't want to refuse.

It was a busy time, but Lynn checked on me periodically to make sure I was OK. Without my notebook, my entertainment was eavesdropping on the table behind me.

They were talking about guys they'd gone to high school with. "He's got the kind of physique that always looks young," one of them said, and I surreptitiously looked behind me. There were two men there, drinking beer. They were stocky, wearing plaid shirts, and had probably gone to high school in the 70's. Neither had the physique that always looks young.

I had tuned them out and was watching the TV when I heard the quieter one say, clearly, "They're pretty droopy for a factory job."

What could they possibly be talking about now?

"Whaddaya mean, you didn't notice?" the loud one burst out. "She held it up for three minutes — per boob!"

The other man insisted he hadn't seen the items in question.

"Well, if I was the guy who did the job, I wouldn't want her handing out my card. Although she could have stuck it underneath and held it there, they were so droopy."

I couldn't believe what I was hearing. Their dialog was so funny, I asked Lynn if she could bring me a clean napkin and a pen. She brought me a pad of post-it notes instead.

More customers came in, but my section of the bar stayed empty. Lynn stopped by periodically to chat, and so did the other waitress, Stacy, and her husband. I watched Stacy amble over to a customer at the bar and start eating his french fries. She was pregnant.

Lynn came back again. "You must be here on business," she said. I admitted that I was in Summit because it seemed like a quiet place to write, and that I was staying next door.

"Are you going to write about us?" Lynn asked. I looked away, smiling mysteriously. "Yup."

She laughed, wondering if I was joking.

"Are you going to be here for our big Fog Festival next weekend?" she asked.

"No, they've already rented my apartment out for the festival."

She thought for a moment. "Hmmmm, I wonder if we could find someone...heck, by then, you'll probably know someone you can stay with! It's sure gonna be a party."

I could hardly believe my ears. After the morning's über-chilly reception at the cafe, I had decided Summit was a tough nut to crack. Now Lynn was practically handing me the key to the city.

I told her I had noticed the sign coming into town that said "Population 267." "I'm gonna make it 268 for a week," I said.

"We should go out there and change the sign," she said.

I waved one of her post-it notes at her, and said, "I have just the thing to do it!" We giggled.

I finally said I had to go, because I'd smoked enough. I waved my hand, indicating the thick second-hand smoke.

"You have to come back later, when it's not dinner hour, and there's more time to talk," said Lynn. "Did you notice those two guys down there, who had one beer and left?" I hadn't noticed them, and I said so. "Well, you know, a young woman like you, here alone...they were looking over here and asking who you were."

I was incredulous. The lights were awfully dim, but how could they be calling me a young woman? I guessed there weren't quite enough women in Summit.

Next time, it would say "Margaret."

"Here —" Before I left, Lynn wrote her name on a post-it note, along with the location of her antique shop on the main street.

"What's your name?" she asked me. When I told her, she showed me her order pad. "Instead of table numbers, we just write people's names, because we know everyone here." On my order, it said, "Girl at bar." I found "girl" almost as flattering as "young." Even better, I knew the next time I went in, my ticket would say "Margaret."

Back at the apartment, I worked all evening, and started yawning at 10:30. All I wanted to do was go to bed. But if I wanted to see the bar in full swing, I had to go back now. I put on my jacket and dragged my butt out the door. This time, I tucked my notebook into a pocket, just in case there was another awesome eavesdropping opportunity.

When I walked in, the mood had changed. People were playing pool and foosball, most of the seats at the bar were taken, and the cigarette smoke was thicker. The three people behind the bar were definitely part of the party.

I slid onto a bar stool and caught Lynn's eye. "I'm back," I said, stating the obvious. "Great!" she said. She remembered what I'd been drinking, and brought me another bottle of hard lemonade. To my right, a busty woman in a hospital scrub top was sitting between two men, flirting with both of them. They called Lynn over, loudly. "We need some shots here! We're gonna do a toast."

"What are we drinking to?" she asked.

The woman answered, "To 'Men are pigs.'"

"Yeah," slurred one of the men. "Men are pigs."

The other man said, "You have to toast with us, Lynn."

"OK, but she gets to toast with us, too," she said, buttonholing me and dragging me over to the group. She made the introductions — Chris was the tall, gangly one, and Jerry was the one who looked like Clark Gable. Amanda was the woman between them.

Lynn got out a couple of bottles and made a Summit Soaker for Amanda, a shot of cherry Shnapps dropped into a glass of some sort of high-caffeine soda pop. "This is our special drink," she said. "You have to try one." When I looked uncertain, she said, "On the house," and made me one, too.

I actually didn't want to drink to "Men are pigs," because I didn't agree with the sentiment. I just wanted to see what the Summit Soaker was like. It was so sweet, it made my teeth hurt. It wasn't until hours later, lying in bed with my heart racing, that I realized how much caffeine I'd consumed.

There wasn't much alcohol in the Summit Soaker, so I wasn't feeling tipsy at all. I tried to have a conversation with Jerry, but it felt awkward. Conversations are always a little awkward when the other person is drunk and you're not. He finally left to hang out by the pool table, and my nearest neighbors were Chris and Amanda. There was some serious flirting going on between the two. She'd spilled a drink on herself, and now she held the neckline of her blouse away from herself, trying to get it to dry.

Suddenly, she said to Chris, loudly, "For educational purposes, tell me, are these small?" I wondered if the man who'd inspired the "Men are pigs" toast had insulted her breast size.

Chris couldn't believe his good luck. He peered down inside her blouse with evident delight, but his answer was not definitive. Their conversation continued, and the only word I could hear was "tits." Then she showed him again. I lost count of how many times I looked over and saw the two of them like that, his face in the neckline of her blouse.

She was having so much fun with the technique, she decided to take it to the rest of the bar. She pranced off, inviting everyone to look down her blouse and give their opinion.

Lynn came by, rolling her eyes. "She's not usually like this."

Across the room, a man who was looking down Amanda's blouse shouted, "Oh my GOD!"

"Tell me, are these small?"

Then Chris turned to me, his eyes glassy. "You know," I said, "when a woman asks that kind of question, there's only one right answer."

He looked a bit puzzled. "You mean, they're big?"

I nodded.

"Are they?"

"I don't know, you were the one looking," I laughed.

"No, I mean yours."

I was taken aback. "This isn't about mine, it's about Amanda's."

"But are they? Big?"

The conversation continued in this vein for a while, despite my attempts to turn it in any other direction. This is another hazard to conversing with drunk people.

Luckily for me, Amanda came back and occupied Chris' eyes for another spell.

Then she flitted away again, and he resumed his assault on my virtue.

"Aw, come on," he said, trying to get me to show my "tits." He didn't seem at all aware that I was 20 years older than him. I figured the alcohol was blurring his vision as well as slurring his speech.

Chris knocked over his drink, and I quickly grabbed my notebook out of the path of the spill. I hadn't taken any notes, anyway. Lynn brought him another drink, and he spilled that in my direction, too. This time, I knocked my notebook on the floor.

I bent to pick it up, and when I sat back down, he was gazing at me admiringly. He slurred something about looking at my ass.

This was becoming ridiculous. The next time Amanda distracted Chris, I slipped out of the bar, glancing over my shoulder nervously as I walked to my apartment next door. I went inside and locked the deadbolt, even though Tina, the landlady, had told me nobody locked their doors in Summit.

I had arrived in Summit for breakfast at 8:30 in the morning. By midnight, I knew nine people by name and another forty or fifty by reputation. I had shared my story of the cafe, which brought out many frank comments about the waitresses there, Bonnie and Jessica. The consensus was that yes, I was a regular after my first visit. There was already a betting pool, with participants wagering whether I could get Jessica to smile in a mere six days. The odds were against it.

I woke up late on my second day in Summit. I lay in bed, torn between the desire to revel in laziness and the need to show my face in the damn cafe every morning. I finally decided that lunchtime was as good as breakfast.

On my second visit to the cafe, I walked in and sat down at the table by the window where I'd sat the day before. The cafe was mostly empty, and Jessica was efficient but unfriendly. I ordered a hamburger, ate it, made a mental note never to order one again, paid my check, and left.

That night, I waited until 11 pm to go over to the bar. I reached the door at the same time as a couple of people wearing black leather. One of them was a burly bearded man on crutches with only one leg. There was a crunching noise, and he looked over his shoulder.

"Hit the pole," he announced to his friend in a gravelly voice. A man in a brown pickup truck had used forward instead of reverse to get out of his angled parking space, and he'd hit the telephone pole in front of the bar. That was all that stopped him from driving into the bar's plate-glass window.

I mentally congratulated myself for my foresight. A few hours earlier, I'd moved my car to the back of the apartment building, because I was afraid that some drunk might hit it.

Inside, I looked around the bar for familiar faces, but the only person I recognized was Lynn. Then, out of nowhere, Amanda pounced on me. "Miss? I just wanted to apologize for my, er, behavior, last night." I laughed it off, saying "You don't have to apologize to me."

But she was serious. "I'm not usually like that. I don't know what came over me," she said. I knew exactly what came over her. Summit Soakers. Beer. And God knows what — or who — else.

I chose a bar stool, and Lynn brought my hard lemonade. "It's quiet in here tonight," she said. There was a couple at the bar on a date, not interacting with anyone else. Amanda was working on two men again, not the same two as the previous night, and using much more restrained tactics. She didn't show her tits to either one of them.

Lynn introduced me to one of Amanda's conquests, a man named Jim who was originally from Seattle. Having started my journey there, I asked Jim how he ended up in Summit.

He'd been married, and his in-laws lived in Summit. He and his wife moved there to raise their family. After many years, they divorced, leaving him rattling around in a five-bedroom house, alone.

A man in a yellow t-shirt came up, curious about the strange woman in the bar. He introduced himself as Ernie, and Jim told me he was Lynn's boyfriend. Then Lynn came over. "She's the lady I told you about — the writer," she said. She told me his name wasn't Ernie, that he was pulling my leg. Even when she told me his real name, I continued to call him Ernie.

Like Lynn, Ernie wanted to make sure I talked to the most interesting people in town.

"She needs to meet Miter," he said. Lynn nodded her agreement, but neither of them could tell me exactly why I needed to meet a man named Miter.

Ernie sent me over to talk with the one-legged man with the gravelly voice, whose name was Trent. The person with Trent was a grim-looking Native American woman with a short haircut who was introduced as Jody. In her leathers, I had mistaken her for another man. She sat at the bar between me and Trent, silently drinking beer and gazing straight ahead at the wall.

When Trent heard that I was a writer, he said, "I read a book once." I thought he was joking, but he wasn't. "It was *Crazy Horse*, in sixth grade. Oh, there was a second one — *Wednesdays With Morrie* or something. I was in the hospital, and someone told me I should read a book. I read that one in —" He thought for a minute, counting on his fingers "— ten days."

He told me he'd gone to school in a class with only three children. The other two were girls, Marley and Missy. The teacher cut out a picture of a racecar and pasted it on the lath wall. Each day, she moved the car one lath for each word they read. Trent's car moved one or two laths a day. "But those girls, they went all the way down the wall, around the room. Twice! Those damn girls lapped me."

Ernie wandered over to where I was talking with Trent. "I'm v-e-r-y curious about you," he said.

Lynn wiped the bar, laughing, "Watch out! When he gets curious about something in the shop, like an engine, he takes it apart to understand it."

I wasn't used to the way the people in the bar moved around, like drifting boats. It was as though they were at a private party, not a commercial establishment. My habit of picking a bar stool and perching on it for the duration was out of place. I started drifting, too.

"Are you going to be here next weekend for the Fog Festival?" Jim asked, when we drifted together again.

I shook my head. "I doubt it. The place I'm staying is rented out to someone else this weekend."

"You can stay with me; I have five bedrooms," he said. My eyebrows must have gone up, because he said, "Everyone here will vouch for me. I'm a nice guy. I'm not a masher."

I had to ask what a masher was.

"You know, someone who takes advantage of a woman against her will."

I laughed. He definitely didn't look like a masher.

Lynn said, "Or you can stay with us."

Ernie wandered over and vouched for Jim. "He's not a masher. But if you want, you can stay in my motor home."

"I could always pitch my tent," I said. "It's set up in my living room right now." I was trying to dry it out.

"You have a tent set up in your living room? I gotta see this!" said Ernie.

Trent and Jody left, and Mitzi, the woman who owned the hardware store, arrived. She ordered a drink and launched into an enthusiastic conversation with Ernie about kitty cats.

Earlier, I had distinctly heard Ernie say, "I *hate* cats."

His girlfriend and their neighbor were the town cat-lovers, feeding all the stray cats of Summit. "The cats have made an actual path between our houses," Lynn told me.

I finally realized that the "kitty cats" Ernie was discussing with Mitzi were not felines, but a popular snowmobile with a leopard-print seat.

I knew I'd been accepted by the group when the gossip started in earnest. The group took turns telling me about all the weird people in town, then moved onto Frank and Amanda, who had left to go another bar.

"He's going through a tough divorce right now," someone said.

"She's a stalker. She leaves notes on guys' windshields," said Ernie. I wondered if he'd received any of those notes.

Lynn was standing with her back to the door, talking about Amanda, when I saw the subject of the gossip walking up to the door. Panicked, I tried to figure out some way to shut Lynn up, but I wasn't fast enough. Amanda burst back in as Lynn was saying, loudly, "I like her; she's really nice." Lynn was so good-hearted, it was no surprise that she would get caught saying nice things about someone behind their back.

Everyone was stunned to see Amanda return. Conversation stopped, and she announced to the room, "Frank got busted!"

"What happened?" everyone asked, in unison.

He'd driven down to the county line, she said, and gotten pulled over by a cop. DUI. We all groaned.

It took me a while to realize that the County Line was another bar, a few blocks down the street. Evidently, I hadn't seen all of the town yet.

"We shouldn't have let him leave right at one; that's when the deputy sheriff starts his shift and goes down there," Lynn said. Everyone turned and looked at me. I had never seen the deputy sheriff, but he lived in the apartment next door to me.

Ernie said, "It's not a good month for Frank. First the divorce, now a DUI."

Jim sat down next to me, explaining, "Frank has a CDL." As a driver for FedEx, Jim's CDL was his livelihood. Earlier, he'd told me that he always walks to the bar, because a DUI would cost him his job.

"So now Frank's probably going to lose his job? Ouch," I said.

The clocks showed 2 am, and Lynn turned on all the lights, causing us to blink and squint.

"I'll walk you home," said Jim. It was only about 50 feet, and completely unnecessary.

"I wanna see the tent!" said Ernie.

Jim suggested that the four of us walk back to his house. I offered to stop at my apartment for a bottle of homemade wine on the way.

"Good, then I can see the tent," said Ernie.

Later, I was sitting at the square kitchen table across from Ernie. It was a strange dynamic, hard to focus on the conversation, because Jim and Lynn were sitting on either side of us, talking about something completely different and unrelated.

For hours, Ernie had been asking me questions, trying to take me apart like an engine, to figure out what I could be writing in or about Summit, South Dakota.

Finally, at about five a.m., he said, out of the blue, *"Zen and the Art of Motorcycle Maintenance!"*

I grinned at him and put my finger to my lips, glancing at the two on either side of us. They hadn't heard him, and I doubted they'd understand the significance. "Don't tell."

He threw his head back and laughed. "I got it! I got it!"

I kept to myself on Sunday, because the bar and cafe were closed. The wind was intense all day, and clouds of dust blew down the unpaved street.

On Monday, the wind was still howling as I walked to the cafe. I kept my head down and shivered, wishing I'd worn a heavier jacket, or at least a hat. When I opened the door, the wind jerked it out of my hand.

I sat down in a booth without attempting to make eye contact with either of the waitresses. I was a regular now. I'd been a regular since my second visit, the one with the regrettable hamburger.

Bonnie came over to take my order. "How are you surviving the wind?" she asked. My eyes were watering, and I admitted that the wind was responsible.

After she took my order to the kitchen, I pulled out a pen and the two postcards I'd been planning to write. Then she came back with the coffee pot. "How do you want your eggs?"

"Over medium, with the toast uncut," I said.

"Over medium, with the toast uncut," she called across the room to Jessica, who had yet to crack a smile in my presence. Bonnie filled my coffee cup, but she still didn't leave.

"So, what are you writing?"

I was sure she wanted to know if it was a book or an article about Summit. She was probably worried that I was going to write about my bad experience at the cafe.

"Postcards," I said.

On Monday evening, I went back to the bar.

"Where were you yesterday?" the owner, Glen, asked.

"I didn't think you were open on Sunday," I said.

He seemed disappointed, "I told you if my truck was here, I'd be here. The back door was open."

I was surprised. I hadn't even been aware that I was invited to a private party.

It was fairly quiet in the bar on Monday. At some point, I decided that Glen liked me, because he kept sidling over to talk. And flirt. Drinks kept appearing in front of me, but I never got charged for them.

He suddenly appeared and asked me, point-blank, "Thong or panties?"

I choked on my drink and squawked, "What?"

He just waited. "Well?"

"Depends on what else I'm wearing." That got his interest. "If it's a long dress, maybe neither."

"Have you got a dress?"

"Sure, a couple of them. I even have an evening gown. In my car."

"You're kidding," he said. He'd seen the miniscule car I was driving, a Geo Tracker with barely enough room for me and one passenger, let alone luggage.

"No, I'm not kidding. It's orange satin."

"Low-cut?" he asked.

"No, backless."

He put another free drink on the bar in front of me. "If you wear it in here, I'll buy you dinner," he said. Our eyes met. It was a challenge.

"I'll think about it," I said. I didn't say what I'd be wearing underneath, but I was considering granny-bloomers or a chastity belt to protect myself.

In the morning, I dug through the luggage in the car. There was a duffel bag on the bottom, full of things I was absolutely certain I wouldn't need until I got home. Inside, I found Santa Claus hats, smiley face light fixtures, life jackets, and bicycle locks. Finally, I saw a hint of orange satin — my elegant evening gown was at the bottom, under the yacht signal flags.

That day, the wind had finally quit, replaced by the insidious fog that would be celebrated by the Fog Festival at the end of the week. I decided I didn't need to go to the dysfunctional cafe for breakfast any more.

The dysfunctional bar was much more of an attraction. It was quiet and not too crowded when I went in after dinner on Tuesday. I knew most of the folks there by now, except for a statuesque woman with an incredibly pale complextion. She was introduced to me as Pinky.

Lynn asked how my writing was going. She still wanted me to meet the mysterious Miter, who hadn't been in the bar all week.

Glen came over to flirt. "That's not an evening gown. You owe me dinner," he said.

I laughed. "You didn't say when I had to wear it."

"Now," he said.

I was challenged, but I stood my ground. "Later," I said. He shook his head and walked away, disappointed.

Later that evening, there was a commotion around Pinky. She had come up with a new form of entertainment, displaying her breasts to one of the men in the bar in exchange for a dollar bill. Lynn gave her some tape, and Pinky climbed up on the bar and taped the money to the ceiling.

Several of the men, including Glen, were pulling out their wallets and looking at me hopefully.

"Nuh-uh," I said, crossing my arms over my chest.

There was some whining and begging, but I stood firm. The conversation turned to what might happen if the entire ceiling was covered in dollar bills. "We could donate all of it to the raffle," suggested Lynn. "What raffle?" I asked.

In the dim bar lighting, I hadn't even noticed a large rifle behind the bar, hanging over the beer cooler, under a handwritten sign that said "WIN ME." They were raising money for a project at the local school.

"You're kidding! You're raffling a gun in a bar to help little kids? Only in South Dakota," I said, incredulous.

"I'll buy one of those tickets," said a guy I didn't know, who hadn't put his wallet away. That's when Lynn realized that the raffle organizers hadn't given her any paper tickets to sell. Rummaging behind the bar, she found a stack of cards with photographs of scantily-clad women on them. She wrote the man's name and phone number in the margin and dropped the card into an empty liquor box.

Around 11 pm, the bar was settling down. There were only a few people there, and I was comfortable with all of them. When Glen put a free drink in front of me, I decided it was an acceptable bribe. I took a couple sips and then slid off my barstool.

"I'll be right back," I said.

I could feel everyone's eyes on my back as I walked out the side door, the one that faced my apartment building.

I brushed out my long red hair and put on the backless dress, some matching earrings, and a tiny bit of lipstick. From the ankles up, I looked great. However, I had a dilemma.

The only shoes I had on my trip were sneakers and hiking boots, which completely ruined the effect of the elegant dress. I padded around the apartment, barefoot, trying to figure out what to do. When I looked at myself in the full-length mirror, I decided I would probably freeze, but barefoot looked good enough.

I trod gingerly across the gravel alley, hoping nobody would see me and that I wouldn't pick up a sliver of glass. Then I took a deep breath and walked back in through the side door.

Lynn noticed me right away and clapped her hands excitedly. "Look at that!"

In my floor-length orange satin dress, I practically glowed in the dark. Every single person in the room except me was wearing jeans and sneakers or boots. The guys had their standard grungy baseball caps, and Ernie was wearing a black mechanic's jacket with his (real)

The barefoot redhead in the orange evening gown

name on it. Pinky had on faded jeans and a baggy, plain white t-shirt. I felt foolish, as if someone was playing a joke at my expense.

Everyone stared at me. Conversation stopped.

I blushed with embarrassment, but I put on a big fake smile. "Hey, let's get a picture of us together," I said to Lynn, holding out my camera. Glen didn't have much to say. He just kept staring at me, as if he couldn't believe he'd lost the bet.

By the time the evening was over and Lynn turned on the bright lights, I had posed for photos with Lynn at the bar, with Glen by the jukebox, stretched out on the pool table, and sitting on top of the bar in front of the gun. Pinky briefly stole the limelight by showing her breasts again and taping a second dollar to the ceiling.

On my last night in town, I went to see Glen about the bet, and the dinner he owed me. Lynn had the night off, and Stacy and her husband were arguing behind the bar. Their squabbling made me uncomfortable.

"I have to interview a new waitress," Glen said, "but then we'll talk." He gave me a significant look.

I ordered a drink from Stacy and waited. The place was mostly empty, and quiet.

A slender, dark-haired woman came into the bar and asked for Glen. They shook hands, then stepped a few feet from the bar to conduct the interview. I had heard that she worked at a bar in a nearby town and was looking for additional part-time hours.

What happened next disturbed me. Glen asked her a question, and as she began to answer it, he bent his head closer to hers to hear the answer. He seemed to be looking at her cleavage, instead of her face. Then he casually slid his arm around her waist. She didn't react. As I watched, his hand slid lower, and lower, until he was slowly massaging her derriere.

She continued to answer his interview questions as if sexual harassment was a normal part of job-hunting.

I put some money on the bar and left without saying goodbye.

I'd stayed long enough to do what I set out to do. I'd met dozens of fascinating, interesting people and made friends with some of them. I'd gone from anathema to receiving decent service at the cafe. In my quiet apartment, I'd even gotten a fair amount of writing done.

It was time for me to quietly slip out of town and move on.

I'd made more of an impression than I intended. I suspected that the folks in the bar would remember the barefoot redhead in the orange evening gown, that crazy, mysterious writer with the spiral notebook, for a lot longer than they would remember Pinky's two dollar bills on the ceiling.

CHAPTER 14

REAL PEOPLE ARE NOT A TOURIST ATTRACTION

The places that are the most beautiful and have the most interesting history are the most frustrating places for me. Unlike Summit, South Dakota, they are overrun by tourists.

When tourists come by the busload, the local people become weary. They don't want to interact with yet another stranger asking the same dumb questions and making the same dumb observations. So they keep everyone at arm's length, holding only brief polite conversations in order to sell us something, to separate the strangers from as much money as possible.

When I lived in Seattle, I was sometimes one of those weary local people. I coined the pejorative term "touron," for tourist + moron, because visitors toting shopping bags full of Space Needle t-shirts clogged my sidewalks and got in the way of my grocery-shopping. If only they would recognize that real people lived in Seattle, people who couldn't dawdle and gawk, who needed to quickly buy a week's worth of produce at the Pike Place Market on their lunch hour!

Then I went 3,000 miles away, to Hilton Head Island, and I found myself on the other side of the equation.

The local people of Hilton Head wanted to politely keep me at arm's length. They'd had their share of "tourons."

Barry and I didn't choose to go to Hilton Head, specifically. That was just where a sailboat, with the head-scratching, misspelled name of *Falcon Rougue*, was moored when we found her for sale on the internet. The process of buying and outfitting the boat — and coming up with a more appropriate name that Neptune would find acceptable — took a few weeks. During that time, I discovered that there were actually *two* Hilton Head Islands.

There was the one that the tourists experienced, a perfect place with beautiful beaches, where smiling people rented bikes and pedaled along many miles of smooth, level bike paths. It had gourmet restaurants and gourmet grocery stores and many, many liquor stores. There were rambling little shopping malls full of clever little boutiques, selling clothing and jeweled flip-flops to people with perfect hair. Their expensive cars had personalized license plates from northern states that said things like BCHLOVER.

The zoning in this Hilton Head was so tightly scripted that even Wal-Mart and McDonald's and Wendy's hid behind small, tasteful wooden signs, and their parking lots were full of trees and bushes to disguise the storefronts. I once turned off the main road into a parking lot with a Staples sign, then got lost in the landscaping and spent over ten minutes trying to find the entrance to the office supply store.

My challenge was finding the *other* Hilton Head, the one with local, colorful folks. They may be shy, like my human chipmunks, or they may be bold, but if they thought I was a touron, they would hang back. They would check me out thoroughly before even trying to have a conversation.

For weeks, Barry and I were driving around in a rental car, trying to solve the boat's engine problems, plumbing problems, electrical problems, and mechanical problems. During those weeks, we got to know some very interesting human critters, some shy, some bold. Some were downright tragic.

Hilton Head was a pretty small town, with a permanent population of 40,000. That figure included a lot of "Come Heres," people who retired from somewhere else in order to support the clever boutiques and liquor stores. If you subtracted them out, the number of *colorful* local people was much smaller.

Walking back and forth to my boat, which we had just named *Flutterby*, I always passed a shrimp boat called *P.I.F.* It was old and worn and a little grubby, the only working vessel in a marina full of shiny sportfishing boats and sailboats.

Several times a day, I chatted with the owner of *P.I.F.*, a garrulous, wisecracking fellow named Billy. When I asked about the acronym, he laughed at me for not knowing that it stood for "Paid In Full."

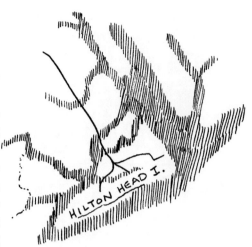

There's only one road to Hilton Head.

He and his girlfriend, Mary, would go out overnight on the boat and come back with the freshest, biggest shrimp I've ever eaten.

"You gotta cook 'em with the heads on," he told me. "The flavor's better." I wasn't sure if that was true, or if he just didn't want to bother removing the heads.

The shrimp tasted great, but their big black googly-eyes were disturbing. What was more, with the heads on, I struggled to round up the antennae and wrestle them into my small cooking pot. They reached halfway across my galley.

The longer we stayed at the marina, the longer Billy's conversations with me became. Instead of dreading the long walk to the bathroom, I began to look forward to walking past *P.I.F.*

She was staring at the bridge.

Billy shared stories about the real Hilton Head, and he told me what went on behind the scenes. He always had some hilarious tale to tell about the local people.

Billy told me that he and Mary were not particularly compatible, but, "You know how it goes…" His voice trailed off. I had certainly noticed how the two of them went on benders, screeching drunkenly at each other so loudly that the entire marina could hear them.

Out of the blue, Billy started talking about the high bridge that arched over the creek next to the marina. It seemed like a non-sequitur, but then he returned to the subject of Mary. He said that a couple of years previously, she had been his best friend's girlfriend.

There was a pause, and then Billy told me his best friend fell to his death from the bridge.

I was taken aback. "What? That bridge, right there?" I asked. Suddenly, I noticed how close it was, and how loud the traffic on it was. The bridge dominated the horizon.

"Yeah," said Billy. He and Mary had gotten together to console each other.

I had seen Mary sitting in their car in the parking lot for hours, not doing anything, just staring out into space. The bridge dominated the parking lot, too.

Meanwhile, I was running errands on Hilton Head each day to get our new boat outfitted for the trip north.

In the auto parts store, I met Tommy, the fastest-talking southerner I've ever heard. He had such a sarcastic sense of humor, I couldn't tell if he was being nice or mean. But I just kept going back to see him over and over as we needed more and more parts. I decided that he was definitely nice, even if he wanted people to think otherwise.

For ten days, Barry and I had been trying to figure out how to get a small piece of exhaust insulation, something that's always sold in gigantic, expensive rolls. I finally brainstormed with Tommy about it in the auto parts store, and he told me to talk with a fellow named Buddy. He then reeled Buddy's phone number right off the top of his head — which amazed me, until I found out they were brothers. Buddy was the "boat guy," and Tommy was the "car guy."

On the way back to the boat, I stopped — of course — to chat with Billy, who by now called me Miss Margaret, a polite form of address used in the old South. It turned out that he knew both Tommy and Buddy, having grown up with them. He told me to go see Buddy right away, saying "He's got a spool of that insulation right on his work bench for ya'."

I hesitated a little, because we had spoken with another mechanic about the problem, and I didn't want to waste Buddy's time.

Billy reassured me, saying that I didn't have to hire Buddy, just talk to him. "You know the difference between being committed and being involved?" he asked me. "When you sit down to a plate of bacon and eggs, the chicken was involved, but the pig was *committed!*" He laughed and laughed.

I finally figured out that Buddy's boat shed was the huge mysterious building next to the marina parking lot. The answer to my

"The chicken was involved, but the pig was committed!"

insulation dilemma had been right there all along, just a few feet from my rental car. But like feeding a chipmunk, I had to hang out and be patient. Buddy wasn't available to help just any tourist from the northern states.

I almost blew it, though. When I first saw Buddy, he looked so much like his brother, I thought Tommy had driven over from the auto parts store. When I blurted out something about the resemblance, Buddy was not amused. He threatened to kick me out of his shop!

Buddy was even more sarcastic than his brother, so I couldn't actually tell if he was serious. At least he talked more slowly, so I could understand him about 90 percent of the time (as opposed to 50 percent with Tommy). He gave me a really good deal on the insulation but made fun of me for only using 10 feet of the giant roll.

Afterwards, I couldn't walk back down the dock without reporting to Billy about what happened and showing him the prized piece of insulation. I was proud, but also sad. The insulation was the only thing keeping us from departing. Now we could leave, but I didn't want to.

I wanted to stay and get to know the people, those interesting local critters who had finally come out of their hidey-holes and decided that I wasn't an average "touron" from the North. There was an underground network on Hilton Head that had been talking about me, and they decided I was "OK."

Now, when I visit a place that has a lot of tourists or business travelers, I take it as a special challenge to connect with the real people who live there. Those people can be open to conversation with strangers, but I have to have something more interesting to say than the last 5,000 visitors they interacted with.

CHAPTER 15

I MET THIS CRAZY LADY ONCE
(AND SHE WAS ME)

In addition to "Never take candy from a stranger," my parents told me, "Never get into a car with a stranger." That's a rule I've broken more than a few times, always with interesting results.

I once arranged to ride to a picnic with a woman named Sandy, whom I'd never met before. When she arrived at the marina to pick up me and Barry, there was another passenger, who was introduced to us as Joanie, in the front seat. As soon as we got on the road, the four of us found that we had a lot in common, and there was plenty to talk about during the hour-long drive. The conversational ball was never dropped; we took turns swapping lively stories all the way from Brunswick, Georgia, to Crooked River state park.

It was as we were getting out of the car that Joanie gave me this epiphany: "In life, you never know when you're going to become someone's story."

I suspect I have become someone's story more than a few times. I'll never know how many.

"Isn't it weird that there's such a big pile of snow in the middle of the road? You'd think they'd plow it over to the side," I said to Barry, as I carefully swerved around it. The road past the pile of snow was not really plowed, but the surface was well-packed, so our 2-wheel drive Honda had plenty of traction.

We drove on for a little while in silence, enjoying the deep green pines on either side of the road, their branches accented with fluffy white snow.

"I hope this shortcut wasn't a bad idea," I said. "I wonder why they didn't plow this part of the road?"

The snow was getting a little deeper, still pretty well-packed, but I had to concentrate to avoid skidding. Eventually, the snow got deep enough that we considered going back, but where would we turn around without getting stuck in the snow? Doggedly, I drove on.

Finally, we reached an impasse. The road was blocked by a man-made snow berm all the way across. As I rolled to a gentle stop, I could see the main highway just on the other side, and it was completely clear of snow!

As I took this in, I saw two men on the far side of the berm, unloading snowmobiles from a trailer. They stopped and stared at us, incredulously. Here we were, in the middle of Oregon, up to our ears in snow, but instead of skis, we had a giant aluminum canoe tied to the top of our tiny car.

We were the most interesting thing they had seen all day.

I got out of the car to look more closely at the situation. One of the guys walked over, and we faced each other across the 5-foot high snowy roadblock. He looked like a local farmer in his plaid flannel jacket.

"Well," he drawled, with a wry smile, "I jest don't think Peepcar is gonna make it over that." He'd noticed the name on our personalized Virginia license plate. "How'd ya end up on the snowmobile trail?"

I was moving tiny spoonfuls of snow.

I looked over at Barry, sitting in the car, and we burst out laughing. That explained why this particular road was so snow-covered!

I rummaged around in the back of the car and found our only shovel, a tiny green folding foxhole shovel. We'd bought it in case we camped someplace without a toilet. Gamely, I walked up

"I jest don't think Peepcar is gonna make it over that."

to the berm and began trying to clear enough snow to get the car over it. It was like using a teaspoon as earth-moving equipment.

On top of that, Barry couldn't help; he was recovering from a broken leg and wasn't permitted to do anything strenuous. He sat in the passenger seat, watching me.

The two guys with the snowmobiles also watched for a moment or two. Then their chivalry got the better of them, and they came over to where I was moving tiny spoonfuls of snow.

I explained why Barry wasn't able to help, so they pitched in. Since they didn't have a shovel, either, they tried using their heavy boots to kick the snow down.

Progress was painfully slow. The snowplow folks had deliberately piled an awful lot of snow here.

"This ain't working," said one of the men. "I'm going to try running my machine over it, gunning it at the top to throw a bunch of snow out of the way." His friend nodded in agreement as he got on his snowmobile and did just that. The snow flew out behind him, and when he reached the other side, the berm was a few inches shorter.

It only took about ten minutes for them to clear three feet of snow that way. Then Barry got behind the wheel of the car, and with the three of us pushing, we shoved the car over the remaining hump of snow. We thanked the snowmobilers profusely and drove away, our distinctive silver canoe reflecting the sun from the top of the car.

We've recounted the story of Peepcar and the snowmobilers dozens of times over the two decades since then. It's always good for a laugh.

But what about those two guys with the snowmobiles? They'd planned a fun time that afternoon on their snowmobiles, but I'd wager that's not the part they remember. It was the crazy kids with the canoe who made the day memorable.

For all I know, every time they go snowmobiling at Diamond Lake, they still say to each other, "Remember that time we rescued the kids with the canoe on this trail?"

I usually try not to do things that are dangerous or stupid. Nonetheless, I am known for things that make me more likely to become someone's story. I do things that are creative, artistic, colorful, maybe even crazy or weird. I strive for goofiness.

I was craving coffee one morning as I drove through Zanesville, Ohio, with Philip. I had been thinking of getting a cup to go, but when I drove past an old-fashioned donut shop, I had a better idea. We parked and walked inside the place, the only customers. Decorated with a lively visual overload of Ohio State football memorabilia, it seemed like an excellent place to drink coffee, and eat highly caloric, sugary pastries.

We ordered a couple of lattes and donuts, and while the woman behind the counter was making our drinks and getting our donuts out of the case, I elbowed Philip and showed him what I had in my pocket, a red clown nose. He grinned at me, because he had one, too.

We put them on while the woman had her back to us, making our coffee drinks and ringing up our order.

When she turned towards us, she nearly dropped the cups.

"Oh my God, it's a couple of clowns!" She was hooting with laughter as Philip paid for our order.

For the donut lady, we became a story immediately. As soon as Philip and I sat down at a table across the room, she picked up her phone to call a coworker.

"Come back over here! You have to see these nuts before they leave," we heard her say.

By the time the second woman arrived, Philip was attempting to wear *two* clown noses at once. Of course, they weren't designed for that, and both of them tumbled into his latte, splashing coffee all over his favorite shirt and causing him to flee to the bathroom in dismay.

"You have to see these nuts before they leave."

The donut-shop employees laughed uproariously. The goofy people with clown noses made their day.

On one memorable drive across the country, Barry and I traveled with four inflatable space aliens in the back seat of the Squid Wagon. They were pink, green, blue, and purple, and at four feet tall, they were the size of large children. Since inflatable space aliens are made to be hung up as decorations, their necks were too weak to hold their heads up. So each one wore an eye-catching pink duct-tape collar trimmed with shiny silver mylar.

Their little bodies were so skinny, I was able to strap all four into the rear passenger seat with one seatbelt. For weeks, their giant almond-shaped eyes peered out every time we opened the side door of the van. They were visible to the public many times a day, every time we stopped at a park, a rest area, a campground, a restaurant, or a store.

I was shocked at the number of people who simply walked past them without saying anything. Did they notice? How could they not comment on something so weird?

The strangers who did stop, however, were always fun and interesting. Our inflated passengers inspired some lengthy conversations, and in one situation, made a lasting impression on a Good Samaritan.

How could they not comment on something so weird?

The four "girls," as we called them, were with us when the Squid Wagon broke down on the side of the road in the middle of nowhere, also known as Iowa. It was Sunday, and there wasn't a human being for miles. For the first half hour, while we were scratching our heads, arguing about what to do, not a single car passed us. Then a diesel mechanic named Tim appeared, seemingly out of the sky.

Tim stuck his head under the hood with Barry, confirmed the problem, and spent 40 minutes trying to jump-start the van from his truck. Finally, he drove back to his shop, got something to help the engine turn over more easily, came back, and jump-started it. He hung around for a little while, talking with us, while we made sure it didn't die again.

As he was about to leave, I asked him to wait. "I want to give you something for your trouble," I said. He shook his head, afraid I was trying to offer him money. But Barry knew what I had in mind. "You're going to like this," he told Tim.

I walked back to the van and selected one of the space aliens as a surprise for his kids. He was grinning like a kid himself as he drove off with the one we'd named A. LeeAnn in the front passenger seat, strapped in with her own seatbelt.

I'm not advocating that everyone travel in a breakdown-prone van with a bunch of inflatable space aliens for passengers. Or that everyone drive on snowmobile trails. Or that everyone walk through the Seattle airport wearing flashing, blinking fur-trimmed bunny ears (Yes, I have done this. It was not even on Easter.).

There are less-goofy ways to become someone's story.

I once stepped out of a library in Jacksonville, Florida, and stopped in my tracks. There was a woman standing a few feet away, with her back to me, and it was like looking at the back of myself: Her remarkable waist-length, strawberry blonde hair was the exact same color and length as mine. When she turned around, she stared back at me in surprise.

Then she walked over to me, and she held out a handful of her hair. When I held a handful of mine next to it, we both studied it with amazement. It was absolutely identical in length, color, and texture. We burst out, simultaneously, "Twins!"

We started talking, starting with our hair, but soon we found that we had many other things in common. Michelle and I were the same age; our birthdays were only a few days apart. She had once lived aboard a sailboat, and I currently lived aboard one. We had family roots in Jacksonville. We were spending our days in the same library.

Eventually, after a half an hour of conversation, we began to explore our differences. That's when Michelle admitted why she was hanging out in the library.

She and her boyfriend were homeless, sleeping in the adjacent park.

Michelle owned a car, but it had been stolen and found 1,000 miles away. Without money to go to Virginia and retrieve it, her car might as well have been found on the moon.

Her boyfriend had a low-paying job, but he was saving all his money to get his car running again. Health problems made it hard for Michelle to walk, and since the nearest fast-food restaurants were a half-mile away, she was hungry. She'd spent the last of her money to fill a prescription that day.

I rode my bike to Burger King and bought her some dinner. When I brought it back, I sat with her on the grass in the sunny park while she ate. I felt helpless in the face of so much misfortune, but I recognized that my company was as important to Michelle as the food. It reinforced her dignity; we looked like two sisters having a picnic.

Sometimes, when people comment on my beautiful hair, I think of Michelle, and I share her story. Michelle's hair was just as beautiful as mine, even though she had to wash it in the public bathroom sink.

Twins!

CHAPTER 16

TAGGING ALONG WITH EXPERTS

When I was growing up, I received a mixed message. There was the standard, "Don't talk to strangers," given to me by my mother, father, and a whole slew of older brothers and sisters. Meanwhile, I saw my father breaking the rule constantly. He was always talking to strangers! As a journalist, he had an excuse, a professional reason to gather their stories. I couldn't wait to grow up and be allowed to talk to strangers, like Dad did.

He recently told me about a breakfast picnic he'd had the previous week with a friend. They were sitting in a waterfront park in Sarasota, Florida, sharing coffee cake and fruit, when Dad struck up a conversation with a park employee who was emptying the trash containers. Dad, who is in his late 80's, went on to relate dozens of crystal-clear details he'd learned in talking with this stranger.

He painted an elaborate word-portrait for me of a couple who had retired to Florida from well-paying jobs in the north, got bored, and went to work again, he as a park maintenance worker and she as a meter maid. "I asked him if he had any hobbies," said Dad, "and he said his grandchildren were his only hobby."

If you asked me what my Dad's hobby is, I'd say "talking with strangers."

They got bored and went to work again.

I know many people like my Dad, who can strike up a conversation with anyone. They are experts in talking with strangers. They set aside judgment and launch themselves into the world with huge smiles and big gifts. In return, they get huge smiles and big gifts back.

I love tagging along with these experts, learning how they do it.

Some, like my big brother Hank, mistakenly think they are tagging along with me. I know, however, that the reverse is true. I hang around with Hank to learn new ways to talk with strangers, tactics and techniques that I haven't tried before.

When I arrived at his apartment in Ohio, ready to take a week-long driving vacation together, he handed me a brand-new toothbrush in its original packaging. "Here," he said, "I got one of these from my dentist last week, and he said to give you one, too!"

I've never met Hank's dentist, so why would he send me a toothbrush?

The answer is my brother's infectious enthusiasm. He'd been living in anticipation of our road trip for months, talking about it with everyone he met. It's no surprise that his dentist would send me a bon voyage present.

Or maybe he just knew that traveling with Hank, people would see my teeth, because I'd be smiling a lot.

Hank and I had never gone on vacation together, just the two of us. I was apprehensive about taking responsibility for someone who seems healthy and strong, but is actually very fragile. Hank, who is visually impaired and developmentally disabled, told me he'd recently had an epileptic seizure. He went to the bathroom in the middle of the night and woke up on the bathroom floor in the morning. What

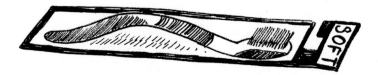

Why would his dentist send me a toothbrush?

would I do if that happened in a motel someplace? The thought terrified me.

Then there was the pressure from people who looked at me like I was some kind of saint. When I explained to my new friends in Summit that I couldn't stay for the Fog Festival because I'd promised a road trip to my disabled brother, one of them said, "It takes a special person to do something like that."

The truth is, I'm not a saint. I'm a hedonist, and I wanted to have a good time. I wanted to see the world through my brother's eyes, to see how he got candy from strangers.

On our first day, at Canadian Customs, the traffic director in the orange vest leaned on my open window for a chat.

From the passenger seat, Hank told him, "My sister is taking me to Canada because I've never been there." When he spoke, the man realized that Hank was special, and he looked at me like I'd suddenly sprouted a halo.

"I have a special needs daughter," he said. "I hope someday her brother and sister will take her on vacation…"

I smiled and said, "You know, it just depends on the example their parents set."

He nodded thoughtfully. "God only gives you what you can handle."

Two days into the trip, it was more than I could handle. My hedonist needs weren't being met. Yes, it was fun, and some fun takes more work than other fun. But this was taking too much! It was the most exhausting travel I've ever done. How could someone so slow make me run so fast?

I found myself crawling on my hands and knees, looking for a tiny dropped pill. I listened through the bathroom door for 10 minutes as he argued — out loud — with the shower curtain, trying to get it to stay inside the tub, then, exasperated, his voice several octaves higher, he hollered for me to help. I unloaded our luggage, carried it to our room, and in the morning, carried it out again. Back on my hands and knees, I checked for lost items under the beds. "Is this your toothpaste?" I asked, finding it there.

I was so busy playing social director, I didn't notice that the fluffy clouds had turned ominous. On our third morning, we awoke to

"Is this your toothpaste?"

high winds and pouring rain. Damn. All my plans had hinged on decent weather.

To buy time, I did what my parents always did — I found a hotel with an indoor swimming pool. I could spend time researching activities for the rest of our week while Hank had something more interesting to do than watch TV. When he found out there was also a hot tub, he was tickled pink.

We unpacked in our room, and I made sure he knew how to find the lobby on his own. He put on his swimsuit and left me to my computer. I promised to follow as soon as I could.

It was almost two hours later that I finally put on my bathing suit and followed him.

When I walked into the lobby, the two employees behind the desk greeted me warmly. "You must be Hank's sister," one said. "He was telling us about your trip."

They knew all the details of our first three days on the road, and the options we'd been considering for the rest of the trip. They chimed in with suggestions, comments about the weather, and news of what had been happening in the lobby and swimming pool

"What did you buy in Canada?"

for the past two hours. It was as though I'd sent a social ambassador over to pave the way for my visit!

I finally relaxed, realizing that no matter what I planned, Hank was going to find people to talk to, and he was going to have fun.

Nonetheless, border crossings always make me nervous. When we drove back across the soaring bridge at Sarnia to Michigan, I was chewing my nails again. That's when I discovered that border crossings were amazingly easy with Hank in the car.

"What did you buy in Canada?" the uniformed Homeland Security officer asked, holding our passports and peering in the driver's window. From the passenger's seat, Hank said, "I bought a t-shirt!" I laughed out loud and admitted that we'd also bought 10 bags of oddly-flavored potato chips. I thought that would surely cause suspicion and a car search. But no, the man just laughed.

"Any alcohol or tobacco?" he asked. "Absolutely none," I said. Traveling with Hank, there was no need for alcohol or tobacco. He was high on life all the time. I loved traveling with someone so genuine, he made guys with guns laugh out loud.

"Hey, Hank, have you ever been to a Hooters?"

"No, but I'll buy you dinner tonight!" Obviously, he knew something about Hooters.

He did notice that their shorts were kinda short.

We had just checked into in a Red Roof Inn outside Detroit, and there were two restaurants across the parking lot from our room: Frisch's and Hooters.

Once inside — I had never been in a Hooters, either — Hank was initially more interested in the baseball game on the big-screen TV than in the waitresses. He did notice that their shorts were kinda short. "What do you call those again?" he asked me. "Hot pants," I told him.

It was loud and lively in Hooters, and after Hank ate his chicken and drank his non-alcoholic beer, I asked the waitress if I could take a photo of the two of them together. "I'll get all the girls!" she said. So she rounded up one of the waitresses, and while she went off to get another one, Hank chatted with her. Then the next one joined them, and he chatted with them both. This went on, adding one waitress at a time, until six of them were gathered for the photo. The picture shows Hank grinning in the middle of the buxom, smiling young women, whom he'd entertained with the details of his big Canadian vacation.

The only problem with Hooters was, they didn't have the sundae Hank wanted. "Let's walk over to Frisch's and see if they have ice cream," I suggested.

He told her all about Hooters.

We walked over to the other restaurant, which was quiet and nearly empty, and the waitress seated us in a booth. She was older than the girls at Hooters, a little overweight, and her entirely polyester uniform consisted of an unflattering polo shirt, slacks, and an apron. I was a little embarrassed when Hank began telling the Frisch's waitress all about his experience at Hooters — not only what he ate there, but how nice the waitresses were.

"The waitresses wear these, um, orange, um, hot pants," he told her. "And I got a picture of me with all of them!"

But by the time he'd finished his ice cream, the Frisch's waitress was sitting with us at our table, enjoying Hank's stories about our vacation and laughing.

That's when I had a little brainstorm, and I asked to take her picture with him. The resulting photo isn't framed on his wall, like the one from Hooters, but I prefer it. Their smiling faces — both Hank and the waitress — are so genuine.

Taking Hank on a road trip was like giving the gift of a smile to everyone along the way. He was so bubbly and happy, it was infectious. That sort of happiness needs to be shared, even if it does wear out the driver.

Another expert at talking to strangers is my friend, Barbara. My favorite story about her also involves a Customs agent at the Canadian border, and some baloney. Or, to be more precise, bologna.

We'd joined Barbara and her husband, Jim, aboard their sailboat for a trip from Seattle to Alaska. It's a 1,000-mile trip through the wilderness with two border crossings, from the US to Canada and back again. Border crossings are a challenge for provisioning. You can't take certain kinds of fruit, vegetables, or meat across the border, so you have to plan your shopping very carefully. And you can count the grocery stores in that thousand miles on one hand.

A year earlier, when Barry and I drove across Newfoundland in the Squid Wagon, we'd picked up a chub of all-beef bologna for sandwiches. I hadn't eaten bologna since I was a kid, but this stuff was excellent. So when I saw the same label in the grocery store in Campbell River, I said to Barbara, "I know bologna has a bad reputation, but that stuff is great." Barry nodded his agreement, and we put it into the cart.

When we opened it the next day, though, it was awful. That's when I read the label and realized it was the same brand, but not the same product. For next couple of weeks, it remained on board but was always bypassed when we made sandwiches. It drifted to the bottom of the boat's refrigerator, forgotten.

We spent the whole day crossing Dixon Entrance under rare sunny skies. Over and over, Barbara ducked into the galley and prepared another plate of fruit for us all to share. I thought she was doing it to celebrate Jim's birthday, but then realized she was carefully using up all the things that we weren't allowed to bring back into the USA.

That evening, when we docked in Ketchikan, a Customs Officer boarded the boat. He was a friendly guy with a clipboard who looked at our documentation and passports. Towards the end of his visit, he asked whether we had any fresh fruit or meat on board. Laughing, we admitted that we had each eaten about ten servings of fruit that day in order to get rid of it. Suddenly, I remembered the bologna and turned serious. "Um, there is some meat on board…some forgotten bologna…we didn't mean to bring it over the border, but none of us likes it. What should we do with it?"

I was hoping that he'd simply confiscate the contraband bologna, but no such luck.

"We don't have an incinerator here to get rid of it," he said, "and you're not allowed to throw it away in our trashcans. I'm afraid that you're going to have to eat it all. Every bit of it."

We all looked at each other in dismay. This was the worst possible sentence! Despite the fact that it would be impossible for him to enforce the law without watching us eat the bologna, I knew we would do as he ordered, because all four of us were law-abiding citizens.

After he left, we gathered our cameras and went into town for a long walk. On the way back, Barbara and Jim lingered to take some pictures, and as Barry and I went down the long ramp to the dock, a man said hello to us. He was lurching and slurring his words, which made me uncomfortable, so I hurried past.

I arranged some fancy cheese and crackers on a plate, and Barry and I sat in *Complexity's* cockpit, waiting for Jim and Barbara to come back for the birthday party. I couldn't wait to see Jim's reaction to the silly birthday hat I'd made for him, a giant paper fish head. Jim had been trying for several weeks to catch crabs, using canned cat food as bait. He hadn't been very successful, and kept saying that what he needed was a nice, fresh fish head.

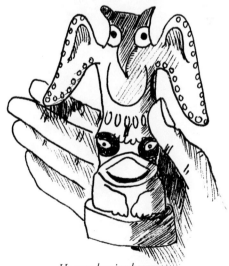

Then I saw Barbara at the other end of the dock, talking to someone on an old wooden fishing boat. We walked over to see who it was, and to my embarrassment, it was the man I'd tried to avoid at the top of the dock. He was showing her some wooden carvings he'd made. She introduced him to us as Frank.

To my surprise and dismay, Barbara invited Frank to come see *Complexity*. He staggered off his boat with a Budweiser in his hand,

He was showing her some wooden carvings he'd made

giving new meaning to "three sheets to the wind" as he followed us down the dock. After looking around and pronouncing Jim and Barbara's boat "nice," Frank sat down in the cockpit with his beer.

Jim went below and got three beers from his special micro-brew stash. "Can I get you anything?" he asked Frank, politely. Frank looked at the bottles in Jim's hand and then at the half-full one in his own. He quickly put his can to his lips and guzzled the entire thing. "I'll have another beer," he said.

Barbara offered him some crackers and cheese, and I slipped down to the galley to see if I could find something else filling and a little less expensive that might soak up some of the excess alcohol in Frank's system.

When I opened the refrigerator, my eye fell on the bologna. I cut it into elegant 2-inch wedges and arranged it on a plate with more crackers. When I brought it up to the cockpit, Frank was amazed. "Wow! Meat! I never get to eat meat!"

As Barbara patiently drew him out with her graciousness and hospitality, Frank told us that his ancestry was half Haida (native) and "half Scotch." He laughed self-deprecatingly and admitted, "Mostly Scotch." Due to his Haida roots, his diet was mostly rice and fish. He made his living as a woodcarver, churning out miniature totem poles for the tourists, but not making very much money. He had a sad life.

I cut it into elegant 2-inch wedges.

Jim said he needed a nice, fresh fish head.

I couldn't wait any longer to give Jim my silly birthday gift. "It's not exactly what I had in mind when I said I wanted a fish head," said Jim, when he saw the two-foot wide cartoon fish that fit over his baseball cap.

As soon as he put the undignified thing on his head, a charter fishing boat pulled up to the dock opposite *Complexity*. Jim quickly left the cockpit — and his gift — and went over to talk to our new neighbors. A couple of minutes later, he returned, grinning, with a plastic bag full of real, smelly fish heads. I was sure my big green fish head had manifested the bait he was looking for. "It will bring you luck if you wear it while fishing," I said. He muttered something politely non-committal like, "Fat chance."

While Frank was distracted by the plate of bologna, not noticing that the rest of us weren't gobbling it with him, Jim won the race for the last beer on the table. When the plate was empty, Frank looked up and asked for another beer. That's when Jim uttered the only lie I ever heard from him. "Sorry, that's my last one."

With no hope of more alcohol from us, Frank wished us good night and wobbled back down the dock to his Budweisers.

Jim turned to Barbara and said, in frustration, "What were you thinking? I was afraid he was going to drink all my beer!"

She shrugged. "He already had one when he started out, so I thought it was safe to invite him down."

"Hey, Frank did us a big favor," I interrupted them.

Jim and Barbara turned to me, surprised. I held up the empty plate. "There is no more contraband bologna on board! We are law-abiding citizens once again, because Frank ate every last piece."

CHAPTER 17

IN OR OUT? THE DILEMMA IN EVERY PARADE

Last month, a man we'd met once, named Ken, stopped by our boat at the marina and tapped on the hull.

"Hi, remember me?" he said, "I just wanted to stop by and see your boat, and to say hello before the parade."

Ken was referring to the Brunswick, Georgia holiday lighted boat parade. He and some friends were going to be in the parade aboard a small racing sailboat called *Jade*. They'd festooned the boat with hundreds of Christmas lights and would be joining a handful of other sailboats to show off for the townsfolk, gathering on the wharf.

We chatted for a few minutes, and Barry and I said we were planning to watch the parade from shore. Ken told us there would be a party afterwards, but he didn't know where. "Give me your phone number, and I'll call you when I find out," he said. We exchanged numbers, and then he had to go, because it was time for the boats to depart.

About five minutes later, he called me. Some folks had changed their plans, and the crew of *Jade* was smaller than expected. Would we like to ride in the parade aboard the boat?

"Absolutely yes!" was my answer. We grabbed our Santa hats and red jackets and headed over to *Jade's* dock. Ken introduced us to the skipper and other crew members, and we slipped our lines and joined the parade. It wasn't a lengthy parade, but it was fun practicing my "parade wave" and getting to know the folks on the boat. Afterwards,

Absolutely yes!

we went to a big party at a local art gallery with everyone from all the boats; it was a fundraiser for the local high school sailing program.

To be a participant instead of a bystander, all we had to do was be ready and say "yes."

The following day, I mentioned our adventure to a woman I met in town.

"I know, I know! I saw you out there in your Santa hat!" she said. She and her family had been in the crowd on shore, watching the colorful, lighted boats as we paraded and pirouetted. She admitted to being envious, telling me, "It was fun to watch, but it looked like the real fun to be had was on the boats."

I had another experience with this when Barry and I traveled across Newfoundland with that expert in getting candy from strangers, my Dad. Each time we ran into someone — admittedly, a rare occurrence on the sparsely populated island in the off-season — Dad would strike up a conversation. We concluded that Newfoundlanders were the friendliest people on the planet, for the people there were willing to stop what they were doing to talk to just about anybody.

In Gander, a fellow en-
tertained us for a half hour
with his charming accent and
witty stories, telling us he had
a "longer tongue than a fur-
lined gaiter." I later figured
out that a fur-lined gaiter was
a type of boot.

It was in the tiny town of
Bonavista that we got to do
more than just talk. Barry and
I joined the local folks in a
once-in-a-lifetime adventure.

We had arrived in town
that morning at the same time
as a yellow school bus loaded
with passengers from a small
cruise ship. "The mayor of this
town has come out to greet

A longer tongue than a fur-lined gaiter.

you," intoned the tour guide as they got off the bus. She wore a lapel
microphone, so her pronouncements were amplified and broadcast
for the entertainment (and eye-rolling) of the entire town. "Here's
Mayor Betty."

The cruise ship passengers formed an orderly line, and each one
dutifully shook hands with the mayor, an attractive blonde woman in
a red jacket. Over the jacket, she wore an elaborate gold chain, not a
mere piece of jewelry, but something that looked very medieval and
royal. "That's my chain of office," she explained to the Americans,
handing each one a pin shaped like a lighthouse that said "Bonavista"
and was probably shipped from China.

Unnoticed by the guide, three independent travelers attached
themselves to the end of the cruise ship line. My father, my husband,
and I wanted to shake Betty's hand, too.

When we reached Mayor Betty, I asked if I could take a picture of her with my Dad. "I've met a lot of mayors in my time,"
said Dad, "but none as attractive as you." Betty threw her head back
and laughed. It was a much more memorable line than anything

Mayor Betty

she'd heard from the cruise ship passengers.

Mayor Betty seemed in no hurry to leave. She gave each of us a pin and gladly posed for pictures. By now, all the cruise ship passengers had vanished, shepherded into a nearby museum by their ever-efficient amplified guide. The four of us chatted for a while about the charms of the town before parting ways in the crisp fall sunlight.

Over dinner that evening, cod cheeks and tongues for me and Barry and fish 'n' chips for Dad, we talked over the unusual events of the day. Mayor Betty was the highlight, although the fried cod cheeks and tongues were exotic enough to be remarkable. We wondered out loud about a strange vehicle we had stopped to look at, parked in the bank parking lot. At first, I mistook it for a trailer loaded with bicycles. Then I realized that it had dozens of seats and handlebars, but only four wheels. On the front was painted "THE BIG BIKE." What did the people of Bonavista use it for?

When our waitress came to clear the plates, she asked us, "Are you going to watch them ride the big bike tonight?" We pressed her for more information, but all she could tell us was that there was a town event planned, and that it somehow involved the bike.

Our curiosity piqued, we drove back to the bank. The parking lot was no longer quiet. It was full of hundreds of people, all milling around the bus-sized red contraption.

We milled around, too, with our cameras, trying to find out what was going on. Everyone was too busy to talk. That is, until we heard a cheerful, "Yoo-hoo! Over here!" It was Mayor Betty, in her distinctive red jacket. She'd left the ceremonial chain of office behind, but she recognized the three of us.

We gave the mayor a report of our day in Bonavista, including the fried cod cheeks and tongues. Then we asked her about the bike.

The Big Bike was a fundraising tool for the Heart & Stroke Foundation. Local teams that had raised money would now be rewarded with a 15-minute ride.

For Betty, this was not an isolated event. Since she'd gotten into office, she had participated in almost every fundraising walk, run, or bike ride in Newfoundland, and as a result, she'd lost over 100 pounds. She wanted her community to get out and exercise, and as the mayor, she was leading by example.

The Big Bike had thirty plain black bicycle seats, ten rows with three seats in each. Every seat had a set of non-steering handlebars and a set of working pedals. It was all mounted on a red metal frame.

The forwardmost seat on the left was for the driver, a man who traveled all over Canada with the bike. He had a steering wheel instead of handlebars, and most importantly, he had the only brake. The bike was equipped with a battery that powered lights and a PA

I understood why Mayor Betty rode with every team.

system with a stereo. The last row had a special seat, actually a raised chair without pedals, where dignitaries could be carried.

I admitted to Betty that I was envious. I would have given anything to ride that bike. But I wasn't eligible. I hadn't raised any money for the Canadian Heart & Stroke Foundation. Heck, I wasn't even Canadian.

The next thing I knew, Betty grabbed us and said, "Come over here." Nobody questioned her authority as she told the organizers that we were the substitute riders for the next team, who was missing some members.

The first thing they did was take a group photo. To this day, I'm sure those folks wonder about the two strangers in red-and-purple hats in their group photo.

Then we clambered aboard the strange vehicle.

I had expected Betty to sit in the rear seat, the one for dignitaries.

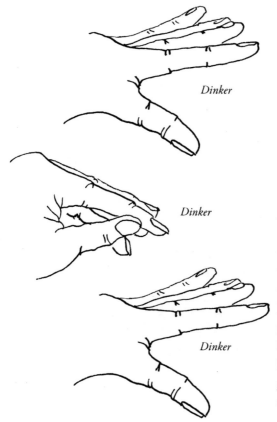

Dinker

Dinker

Dinker

Instead, she jumped on a seat in the front row, next to the driver. "I have to have my hone pedals," she said, in her distinctive Newfoundland accent. You don't lose 100 pounds by sitting and letting others pedal.

Our Big Bike driver first gave us some instructions. Most importantly, the bike had no turn signals. He needed to teach us how to signal turns. "When I shout LEFT, everybody should put their left hand out, like this!" He held out his left hand and began flapping his thumb up and down, saying, "dinker-dinker-dinker," like a car's turn signal. It was the silliest turn signal I'd ever seen, and the silliness multiplied when we all did it at the same time. At every turn, and there were a lot of them, we had to chant "dinker-dinker-dinker" until the turn was completed.

"OK, let's go!" he shouted, cranking up some loud Credence Clearwater Revival on the stereo. I pushed on the pedals, and to my surprise, they barely moved. In front of me, Betty was already cranking away. I grunted and pushed harder, and slowly my pedals began to move. I was working so hard, I barely noticed that the bike was moving now. The Big Bike weighed 1900 pounds, even before we put almost 30 people on it.

Our pace was so slow that neighborhood kids ran along beside us, laughing at our dinker-dinker-dinker turn signals. We didn't mind, we were laughing so much ourselves. The 15 minutes seemed like 15 seconds.

When we coasted back into the bank parking lot, I understood why Mayor Betty rode with every single team. Why would you stand on the sidelines and be a bystander when you could participate every single time?

Sometimes, the chance to participate isn't anything big. Sometimes, it's just jumping in and helping someone do something we've never done before.

Barry and I were walking with our friends from *Complexity*, Jim and Barbara, in a marina in Juneau, Alaska, when we came across a young man mending a fishing net. He had a big pile of net and floats spread out on the dock, and he was using a plastic shuttle to work on them. His nimble fingers were so quick, we couldn't figure out what he was doing by just watching.

Puzzled, we asked him how it worked. He chuckled, because to the uninitiated, it did look like a big messy pile of string. "Here hold this with your finger," he said to Barry. "It's easier with two people."

Barry hooked a finger around one of the strands of the net, and the man began using the shuttle and net twine to make a new sec-

"It's easier with two people."

tion, explaining what he was doing as he worked. We stayed for quite a while, "helping." The work was mesmerizing, but it was easy to talk and get work accomplished at the same time.

Eventually it grew late, and we had to leave. To our surprise, the next morning we found a small gift in the cockpit of the boat. Our net-making friend had left one of the shuttles, with some net and twine and a note that said, "Alaska Souvenirs. Courtesy of F/V *Windbreaker*." Each of the four of us picked it up and studied the functional beauty of the simple plastic tool, the carefully knotted net, and the iridescent aquamarine twine that glowed in the low sunlight.

Now I'm going to contradict myself.

Sometimes, when I want to get candy from strangers, the best way to do it *is* to be a bystander. When the main event is interesting, so are the bystanders.

It's a win-win: If there is something truly interesting going on, I can be *either* a participant or a bystander. Simply finding something interesting that is happening increases my chances of finding interesting people on either side of the equation. The dilemma is how to choose: In the parade, or out of it?

On a hot July fourth, when Barry and I arrived at Riverside Park in Sebastian, Florida, the first thing I saw was a pony ride. We had happened upon a quintessential family-oriented small-town event, with folks of all ages enjoying themselves.

Armed with a picnic and a couple of folding chairs, we plunged into the crowd, our heads swiveling from side to side. There were booths selling everything from airbrushed art to temporary tattoos to cheap imported windchimes. Vendors hawked sausage, ice cream, cotton candy, and Kettle Korn, and roving salespeople had enticing glowsticks, sparklers, and candy for the children.

At the edge of the river, where the fireworks show would be at dark, folks had set up their blankets and folding chairs for many blocks. The orientation was puzzling; the chairs seemed to be aimed every which way.

As we walked along the river, wondering where to have our picnic, we came across a couple of ladies whose chairs were pointing in the wrong direction, facing the throngs of people in the park.

"You must know something nobody else does," I said. "Are they going to shoot the fireworks off over there?" I gestured towards the row of porta-potties that was their view. Chuckling, they admitted their chairs were turned around for conversational purposes. "They shoot the fireworks from that island, at the end of the pier," one of them told me.

Armed with this information, we found a spot right on the river bank, smack dab between the two long fishing piers.

There was a constant parade of people along the waterfront as we ate. One large family wore all red, white, and blue. The kids carried flags and wore headbands with red, white, and blue streamers. Another couple had matching patriotic t-shirts with larger than lifesized eagle heads. I stopped them and asked if I could take a photo, and they posed willingly.

They had set their chairs up almost next to ours, with only one couple between us. We began chatting, starting with the most common question in Florida, "Where are you from?" It's a question that irritates Florida natives, but is vitally important to the northerners who migrate down to the most southern state.

It didn't seem right to talk with Ron and Carol over the head of the woman sitting between us, so we drew Lynn into the conversation, too. It was the seventh year she and her husband, Al, had celebrated the Fourth in Sebastian. They'd been at the park for hours already, "eating too much junk food," she said, just as Al came back carrying the largest bag of Kettle Korn available.

He opened the bag and shared it around, which prompted Ron to get up and buy a second bag of the addictive stuff.

At nine o'clock, the sky grew black with thunderclouds, as if to set the stage. To the west, cloud-to-cloud lightning upstaged the small Roman Candles and bottle rockets that kids were setting off on the beach.

"They'll turn the lights off on the pier right before they start," Lynn told us. As if on cue, the lights went out, provoking a hushed "ooooh" from the crowd.

We had front row, center seats. Not only were the fireworks perfectly centered in front of us, but they were reflected on the still surface of the Indian River, giving us a double display.

The six of us formed a friendly, cohesive group of bystanders, simply enjoying the show together. Surrounded by cheerful, happy people all around us, we passed the bags of sugary Kettle Korn back and forth, eating it by big handfuls. On that Independence Day, Barry and I really did take candy from strangers, and it was sweet.

Taking candied popcorn from strangers.

CHAPTER 18

STAY A WHILE WITH ME

Hospitality comes in all flavors and doesn't have to be elaborate. It can be a simple dinner, like the two guys who entertained me in Chincoteague, or feeding bologna to drunk Frank aboard *Complexity*. When I'm camping, I can share my campfire, and when I'm flying, I can share my snacks (which are usually far superior to the peanuts and pretzels offered by the airline). Whether I am traveling or staying home, I can always find some way to offer hospitality to strangers.

I'm not a member, but I've been inspired by groups like Servas, which has been around since 1948, facilitating hospitality as a way to bring about world peace.

I think keeping people warm is one step towards world peace.

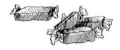

I was on a ferry from Ocracoke Island to the mainland when I noticed a young man standing at the rail, beside a bicycle loaded for touring. He seemed unusually emotional as he watched the island retreat into a small speck, miles behind our wake. He waved farewell at unseen people on shore, receding into the distance.

Joe was only 21, and when I struck up a conversation with him, he told me he was on his first cross-country cycling trip, from Illinois to Georgia. Having lived all his life in the midwest, he'd had some life-changing encounters and experiences during his stay on

Ocracoke Ferry

Ocracoke, including his first swim in the ocean, his first time skinny-dipping, and his first encounter with dolphins — all at the same time! But he was on a fixed schedule with plans to meet his parents in Atlanta, so he needed to continue on his way.

As someone who has traveled long distances on a bicycle, I recognized the hardships he faced on the road, and I knew how important kindness and hospitality were. I told him what he could expect in the next stretch and shared some knowledge of local roads with him. Joe told me that because the weather had become warmer as he rode south, he'd recently mailed his tent back home to save weight. Now he had only a tarp and a sleeping bag.

When I mentioned that I lived on a boat in a boatyard, he was curious; he didn't know anything about people who lived aboard boats, especially in boatyards. So I gave him directions and told him I would be glad to find him a place to stay if he rode to the boatyard that night.

Because I was traveling by car, I would arrive a couple of hours before Joe. I would need that time to unpack; I had not been home in over four months.

Besides unpacking, there were a lot of friends to see when I arrived. Not Barry, though. He had gone on a retreat and would be back the following week.

I went to my friend, Dick, and explained that I had a new friend coming by bicycle. I thought Joe might be more comfortable staying aboard a larger boat, so would it be possible for him to sleep in Dick's spare cabin?

What I didn't say, but Dick saw immediately, was that I didn't want anyone to think I was doing something inappropriate with a young man I'd just met. The boatyard was already full of speculation about why Barry had left right before I returned.

Of course, when he realized this, Dick took advantage of the situation.

He teased me about picking up strange men, about being a cougar, about taking advantage of the fact that my poor, saintly husband was on a meditation retreat. Not only did he ignore my protestations, he enjoyed himself thoroughly, spreading rumors throughout the entire boatyard community. He teased me *mercilessly*.

When Joe arrived, I took him on a tour of the boatyard. I had been eager to introduce him to my sailing friends and answer his questions about the sailing lifestyle, but Dick's teasing took the wind out of my sails. It had never crossed my mind that with my husband gone, we'd be the subject of so many suspicious looks and raised eyebrows.

Nonetheless, I was glad I'd invited Joe to stay, because it was cold that night, and he would have been uncomfortable without a tent. I loved his youthful enthusiasm and enjoyed my chance to vicariously participate in his first big cycling adventure. He was wise beyond his years, a patient listener who took careful notes in tight, tidy script in a pocket notebook.

The only problem was, the two of us stayed up so late, talking aboard *Flutterby*, that I finally just pulled out the settee for Joe and his sleeping bag, and I said good night and went into the forward cabin.

I might as well be hanged for a sheep as a lamb, I thought.

In the morning, after a large breakfast of hot oatmeal, Joe continued his ride south, and I faced the ruin of my reputation with my head held high. After a few months, folks in the boatyard started calling me Meps again, instead of "that cougar."

That wasn't the only time my hospitality provided much-needed warmth to a chilly traveler.

Barry and I had driven the Squid Wagon from Burning Man to Crater Lake for a camping trip with my sister, Julie. We were carrying a lot of extraneous booze in the back of the van.

At Burning Man, we had camped with a large group called the Lamplighters, and we stayed a few days longer than usual to help take down and pack their elaborate camp. Barry and I aren't heavy drinkers, but Burning Man is a leave-no-trace event. So whether it's trash, like a sequin or scrap of wood, or useful abandoned items, like clothing or bottles of booze, we had to make sure everything left the desert. This explains why we were traveling with quite a few large bottles of strange bottom-shelf liquor.

My transition from Burning Man to the default world was very disconcerting that year, and I had a severe case of culture shock. I found myself wanting to hug everyone in the grocery store. I wondered what strangers would think if I started offering them jelly beans and telling them they looked fabulous, as I had done for ten days in the desert.

When we arrived at Crater Lake, Julie had left a note on the bulletin board for us. It said "Meps 'n' Barry, site F12." At the bottom of the note, she'd also written "on-on2." I wondered what that was about.

When we arrived at our site, I asked about the cryptic note. Julie told me that she'd seen another notice on the board that indicated there were Hashers in the campground. Hashers are members of the Hash House Harriers, a worldwide running club that's about 100 years old. Julie had once been involved with the group, who describe themselves as "a drinking club with a running problem."

Their runs aren't very formal or organized, just a leader who takes off with a bag of flour and leaves a white, powdered trail for others to follow. Mostly, they seem to run from beer stop to beer stop, celebrating the end of each run at a pub with more beer.

A few hours later, Julie and Barry and I were sitting at our picnic table, when we heard a crashing through the underbrush, and a couple of people walked into our campsite from the woods. They came into our space as though they knew us, so I figured they knew Julie. Meanwhile, she was thinking the same thing, that they knew me and Barry!

They turned out to be Hashers, drawn to our site by Julie's note. We introduced ourselves and had a grand old time chatting with lively Carrie and Tim.

Finally, as they got ready to leave, Carrie announced that she wanted to do a naked midnight run. "Come by for a drink, if you do. You know we have plenty of booze," I said, thinking she was joking.

After the pair left, Julie turned and gave me a big-sister warning. "Don't offer liquor to Hashers, or you'll never be rid of them!"

The lead runner leaves a white, powdered trail for the others to follow.

We chuckled about it over a late dinner, which consisted of grilled salmon-and-gruyere sandwiches and Cheetos, washed down with a potent fruit-and-rum punch called Goombay Smash. The three of us were having so much fun with our campfire that we didn't notice how late it had gotten. Just after midnight, there was another crashing through the underbrush, and out popped Carrie.

Topless.

All she had on was a tiny mini-skirt and a pair of running shoes.

In true Hasher form, Carrie was carrying a bag of flour, leaving a trail for her running friends to follow. She peered into the woods she had come from, clutching the bag to her bare chest and complaining that none of the losers had actually followed her.

What do you do when a topless woman drops into your campsite at midnight?

Since Barry and I had just come from Burning Man, where topless, as well as bottomless, are commonplace, we were nonplussed. We disregarded her lack of clothing and did our best to make her feel at home.

All she had on was a tiny mini-skirt and a pair of running shoes.

Barry chivalrously added more wood to the campfire, because she was freezing. I got her a glass, so she could add some antifreeze to her system. The Goombay Smash was gone, but there was the bottled Mojito, and beer, and many other mysterious, dusty bottles.

About an hour later, the three of us were laughing and talking around the campfire when a crashing through the underbrush told us someone was finally following the trail of flour. It was Carrie's husband, Tim.

Fully-clothed.

"Where have you been? Where are the others?" Carrie demanded.

The rest of the group had decided it was too cold to be streaking around the campground, so nobody followed her. They figured she'd return quickly when she got cold, not expecting her to find a perfectly good party with a campfire and lots of booze at site F12.

Carrie donned the sweatshirt Tim had brought for her, and lucky for us, they didn't leave right away. His stories were just as entertaining and hilarious as his wife's, so we were glad to extend our hospitality to him, too. Finally, when we started to run out of both booze and firewood, they said goodnight, and he led her back to their campsite on wobbly legs.

In the morning, there was little evidence of our nighttime visitors. We were left with a cold campfire, some empty bottles, and a mysterious trail of white powder leading into the woods. Plus a story that many of my friends accuse me of making up.

Fortunately, there were three of us to serve as witnesses for each other. Because, for the sake of Carrie's modesty, there are no photographs.

CHAPTER 19

INTRODUCTIONS ARE PRICELESS

In the old days, people who traveled carried formal letters of introduction. Before they left home, someone with a connection in the place where they were going would sit down and pen a letter, saying "this is a good person." It might recommend them for a job or ask the recipient to give them a place to stay. The letter proved that this person wasn't really a stranger, she was actually a friend of Aunt Nellie's.

People don't carry paper letters of introduction any more, but introductions are still priceless. They're usually done by email or telephone these days.

When I'm getting ready to take a trip, I make it a point of telling my friends, relatives, and grocery-store checkers where I'm headed, in case they offer to give me an introduction. It's a shortcut, an easy way to meet someone new. An introduction certainly helped when I stopped to see Tina's mother, Shirley, in Spokane.

No matter how tenuous the connection, an introduction can make all the difference between being welcomed and trusted and being ignored. As I had learned on Hilton Head, an introduction can make the difference between being seen as a "touron" and being seen as a real person.

When Barry and I were driving around Newfoundland in the off-season, it was sometimes difficult to find a restaurant that was open. We ran across one in Trepassey that was a converted house. Each of the small rooms had room for only a couple of tables.

Because our tables were so close, we started talking with Mary, a widow from New York who was traveling with her son and his wife. Their clothes and accents were completely American. But Mary told us that she was born and raised on the eastern shore of Newfoundland's Avalon peninsula, part of a very large family.

In the mid-50's, she and two of her siblings had the chance to work on the American Navy base. That's where she met her husband, an American serviceman. When they married, she left Newfoundland to live in the United States, only returning a few times in almost 50 years. Newfoundland was not her home any more; it had been 18 years since her last visit.

Mary told us about the differences between her life in New York and her brothers and sisters who stayed in Newfoundland. When she heard we were heading north, towards Fermeuse, she told us we should look up one of her brothers, Jerome. She described the gas station and convenience store that he owned on the main highway.

A day or so later, we found the place, and I went inside and asked the clerk about Jerome. I mentioned that I had met his sister.

She took me to Jerome's office, where she told him, "This lady is a friend of your sister's." It was the kind of common misconception that makes introductions, even from strangers like Mary, so priceless.

The elderly man at the desk looked surprised. "Oh, do you know my sister from the States?"

"No," I replied, "we just met her two days ago, at a restaurant in Trepassey!"

Jerome invited me and Barry in for a cup of coffee. The three of us sat in the little restaurant, which was closed for the season, looking down at the boatyard and the harbor. Unlike his sisters, he never worked on the base and never left home. His Newfoundland accent

He gazed across at the rows of unused boats in the boatyard.

was so thick, full of "dis" and "dat" and extra s's on the ends of verbs, that I had to interpret much of it for Barry.

The store, which Jerome owned with his son, looked to be a profitable operation. But he admitted that the 90's were "a bad time." In 1992, the Canadian government closed down the cod fishery, leaving many fishermen without a livelihood. "You can't even go pleasure fishing now. If I wants a piece of cod, I have to buy it." The impact was huge for people who ate fish at almost every meal. "Everybody eats chicken now, instead of fish," said Jerome, shaking his head. He gazed across at the rows of unused boats in the boatyard, more sad than bitter.

Many years earlier, before cell phones and internet, Barry and I were driving across the country, and we needed to receive some mail. In those days, we'd use our road atlas to pick a small town

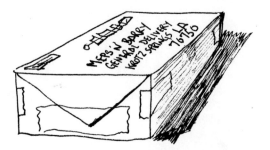

*How long should she hold this
mysterious package?*

in the middle of nowhere, the kind of place that would have only
one post office. Then we'd ask our parents to send our mail there, ad-
dressed to "General Delivery."

This time, we selected the tiny town of Krotz Springs, Louisiana.
When we went into the post office to ask for our parcel, there was
no one there but the postmistress, who was visibly relieved to see us.
Krotz Springs was so small that she knew every person who lived
there. When our parcel had arrived a few days earlier, she was confused and mystified. How long should she hold this mysterious package for two people who had never set foot in Krotz Springs?

We hung around in the post office for over an hour, chatting
and answering her questions about our nomadic life. Finally, as our
conversation drew to a close, we asked if there was a good restaurant
in town. She recommended that we eat at Suzy's, about four blocks
away.

About ten minutes later, when Barry and I walked into Suzy's, the
waitress greeted us with a big smile. "Hi! Y'all are the folks from the
post office, aren't you?"

It was like traveling with Hank as my personal ambassador. The
postmistress had phoned ahead and told the waitress all about us,
our trip, and probably the contents of our mail parcel. Now we were
treated like absolutely royalty in the cafe, and everyone joined into
the conversation with us.

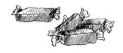

Introductions are not only useful in small towns, but have bridged
the entire Atlantic ocean for us. In 2006, Barry and I decided to

take our first trip to Europe. We had found a boat for sale in Portugal that we wanted to look at, so we bought a pair of plane tickets — super-cheap, because we'd be boarding our plane on Christmas morning.

We bought a guidebook to Portugal and started making lists of the things we wanted to see. About a month before the trip, we stopped to visit a friend, and her door was opened by a serious-looking young man we didn't know. "I am Nelson," he said in careful, accented English. "I am renting a room. Jacqui is downstairs."

We went downstairs, and after she greeted us, Jacqui said, "Did you meet my renter, Nelson? He's a graduate student from Portugal." Barry and I looked at each other, surprised. We hadn't yet told Jacqui of our travel plans.

A few days later, we went to a party and ran into another friend, Janine. "Portugal? What a coincidence! I have a great friend in Lisbon. I'll introduce you in email." She had met Carlos in a chance encounter at a bus stop in Paris and stayed pen pals for over 20 years.

When Barry and I arrived in Lisbon, Carlos met us at the airport, showed us around town, and took us home to stay with him and his father. He loaned us a cell phone and helped us contact the broker who was selling the boat. On our third day, he took us to the bus station and sent us off to explore the south of Portugal, including Portimão, where the boat was located, and the ancient walled city of Évora.

When we returned to Lisbon after our first week of exploring this small country, Carlos welcomed us back for a New Year's celebration unlike any we'd experienced. He told us that he was a little disappointed — most of his local friends had gone traveling over the holidays, so he couldn't introduce us to them. But he was pleased that a number of his other friends, people he didn't see as often, had traveled to Lisbon to celebrate New Year's Eve with him.

It was the most diverse group I'd ever been a part of, with Barry and I being the only Americans.

About 20 of Carlos' friends had traveled from England, Spain, Italy, Brazil, Germany, and Mexico, bringing together many languages, cultures, and personalities. With Carlos as the cat-herder, we spent two happy evenings enjoying Lisbon's nightlife, moving between high-energy bars and cozy, chic restaurants as we communicated in many different languages. When we couldn't find the right words to convey what we meant, we simply resorted to pantomime and hysterical laughter.

By New Year's Day, Barry and I had the hang of travel around Portugal, so we found our way to the train station on our own. We took a high-speed train along the coast to the north, with plans to explore Porto and then go into the interior. Riding old-fashioned trains and buses, we eventually wound our way to the medieval university town of Coimbra.

Carlos, our cat-herder

Nelson met us at our lodgings that evening, and the three of us went out for dinner and then walked around the campus, which dated back to medieval times; it was founded in 1290. We stopped to see the library, and when I asked about the oldest book in the collection, the librarian climbed a ladder and handed me one printed in 1515.

Nelson was only in his 20's, but his somber mien made him seem older. He had completed the coursework for his doctorate and would soon be going before a committee in one of the breathtakingly beautiful medieval chambers to defend his dissertation.

As we walked the streets, I noticed a lot of black fabric in the trees, which were bare of leaves. Nelson had explained that the students often wore long black robes to class, like the ones American

I noticed a lot of black fabric in the trees.

students traditionally wear for commencement ceremonies. We saw students wearing them; it reminded me of a Harry Potter movie.

Nelson said it was not a required uniform, just something many students considered a privilege to wear. It was quick and easy to don a robe over your clothing, or over nothing, when you were running late for class.

When male students were about to graduate, there was a centuries-old tradition where their friends would chase them through town to literally rip the robes off their bodies. The attackers considered it a challenge to throw the discarded robes as high as possible into a tree or to fling them onto the upper-story gargoyles, so that it was difficult or impossible to retrieve them.

Because many students wore their robes with little or noth-ing underneath, Nelson said it was not unusual to see a humiliated young man running home naked after having his robes ripped off and thrown into a tree.

I asked if he'd participated in this sort of thing as an undergraduate.

"Yes," he admitted, reluctantly.

Had he also been a target and had his robes ripped off? To which he reluctantly answered, "Er, yes."

Nelson then became maddeningly silent and refused to provide any further details of the experience. But at least he was smiling as we walked the medieval streets under the fabric-strewn trees.

CHAPTER 20

GETTING OUT OF THE CAR

At a rest area in Idaho, I'd just started the engine of the Squid Wagon when an elderly man getting out of the car beside us struck up a conversation through the open window. He started with a comment about why he loved the electronic key to his car (it kept him from locking his keys inside), then went on to tell us about his life history, the books he'd written, his grandchildren, spirituality, and his thoughts about war and violence. If I had known we'd be chatting with him for 30 minutes, I never would have left the engine running all that time!

He was the exception that proves the rule. Normally, I have to get out of the car to get candy from strangers.

"This is different from what we're used to," I told Paddy, who was sitting on the bench next to me. In Seattle, we get out of our cars for a concert!" He just laughed good-naturedly.

Barry and I were in North Sydney, Nova Scotia, which is the eastern terminus for the ferry to Newfoundland. We had 12 long hours to kill before the scheduled departure of our ferry.

We strolled — slowly — up and down the main street, taking in the aging, mismatched store fronts. We bought ice cream cones, licking them slowly and carefully to make them last as long as possible.

We drove, leisurely, to a farmer's market to buy fruit, selecting only a handful of apples from the piles of potatoes, turnips, and cabbages. We stopped and browsed at a yard sale and spent some time in a playground.

Our slow, deliberate pace made everything seem a bit surreal. And then we ended up in the park, where things were surreal for a different reason.

We were drawn by the sound of music, and we found a concert, with the well-amplified band playing in a small, temporary bandshell. Not Cape Breton's Irish music, which we expected this far north in Nova Scotia, but "cryin' in your beer" country music with a twang. Though the instrumentals were fine, the vocals were off key. Yet it didn't seem to be karaoke.

On top of that, the audience was nowhere near the lonely band. About 50 feet from the bandshell, a handful of people sat on benches. Further out was the real audience: Dozens of cars, with about a hundred people in them, were parked in the gravel lot that surrounded the picnic area, and their occupants were watching the concert through their windshields. I wanted to ask someone why they were sitting in their cars, but they had their windows rolled up!

My curiosity about this strange breed of entertainment led me to Paddy, a cheerful older fellow sitting by himself on a bench. We struck up a conversation, chatting between the songs. I noticed Paddy occasionally looking over his shoulder, and he explained, "I'm waiting for my girlfriend." There was a twinkle in his eye, and I found myself looking around for some matronly older lady who might be heading our way.

But Mary was both younger and more vivacious than I expected. She arrived with her father, 84-year-old Clarence, and we all moved over to make room on the bench. Despite the off-key music, it was a delightful evening, and the five of us chatted and laughed and watched the people. At the end of each number, the cacophony of appreciative honking from the cars was deafening, drowning out both our conversation and our polite applause.

There was a great deal of teasing going on, and I joined in and teased Paddy about his young girlfriend. Mary protested, "I'm a senior citizen!" She told us she'd had her first child at 15, and then went on to have 7 by the time she was 22. She was the youngest great-grandmother I'd ever met.

It was apparent that she enjoyed spending time with her father, who was the first great-great-grandfather I'd ever met. Clarence was short but spry, describing himself as a "jack of all trades, master of none." He had lived his whole life in North Sydney but admitted that he'd never taken the ferry to Newfoundland. Clarence showed us his watch; his now-deceased wife of 53 years had given it to him. When it stopped working, he had the face replaced with her portrait. I could tell how much he missed her presence in his life.

Mary and Clarence had come late to the concert because they were at St. Mary's Catholic cemetery, attending a mass for the dead. They told us that special red candles placed on the graves that night would burn until morning, and that the illuminated gravestones were quite a unique sight, not to be missed. They each had a spouse buried in that cemetery, along with Clarence's father. One of Mary's daughters was murdered 13 years ago in the neighboring community of Sydney Mines. She was in the cemetery, too.

Sipping hot tea, we huddled closer on the bench as it got dark and started getting cold. But we all stayed until the end to hear the band play Clarence's request: "Fallen Leaves," which brought back memories of his late wife. Then we exchanged hugs with our new friends and said our farewells. The cars in the parking lot started their engines, but then sat, stuck in a giant traffic jam as we strolled past on foot.

Barry and I walked back to where we'd parked the Squid Wagon in town and drove to the cemetery, following the directions that Mary and Clarence had given us.

Our way was lit only by the stars and those tiny red dots of light

It was eerie and beautiful. Tiny red votive candles flickered every few feet across the hillside of tombstones. We got out of the van and strolled among them, our way lit only by the stars and those tiny red dots of light. In the darkness, a loon called from a nearby lake, making the hair on my neck stand up.

A few cars drove slowly through the cemetery, using only their parking lights, but after the experience we'd had at the bandshell, it was no surprise that the occupants stayed inside their vehicles. We were the only ones willing to walk, and we had the magic of the candlelit cemetery and the haunting call of the loon all to ourselves.

For decades, I remembered a story my friend, Heidi, told me in high school. She and her family had driven across the United States, along a route that paralleled that of the Oregon trail. She told me how she and her brothers and sisters got out of the car and followed the old wheel ruts from the Oregon trail on foot, meeting their parents and the car further down the road. I was fascinated by the thought that those wheel ruts still existed, etched deeply into the land, 125 years after the trail was in heavy use.

Thirty years later, Barry and I were driving across Nebraska, and we came across a small park with a hiking trail. From the top of a low hill, we could clearly see the tracks of the Oregon trail, carved by thousands of people who passed that way. From the high vantage point, you could see that the trail wasn't one single track, like a road, but consisted of a main route and many alternative routes, places where people went a few hundred feet one way or another.

Standing there, listening to the wind sighing in the grass, my imagination filled the scene with wagons, horses, oxen, and people in the heavy, drab clothing of the mid-1800's. I could also imagine Heidi and her siblings, walking along this route in the 1970's.

We had the place to ourselves except for one other car with New Jersey license plates, and as we stood on the hill, a man joined us at the top.

He was a newly-retired schoolteacher, celebrating his retirement by driving across the country to enjoy the scenery and visit friends. The three of us fell into a natural, easy conversation, the kind you have with someone it feels like you've known for a long time. Eventually, we made the short hike back down the trail together.

We said our farewells and went to our vehicles, but as Barry and I were getting out water and food for a picnic, George came back over to us. In his hand, he held two colorful beaded necklaces.

Murray beads

"I used to make these beads to reward the students in my classes; I call them Murray beads." I chuckled; in the course of our conversations, he'd told us about Murray. That was the name of the giant 1,000-pound ball of aluminum foil he'd created in his classroom over many years as a teacher.

His Murray beads were beautiful. Made from colorful marbled polymer clay, they were perfectly round, strung on a navy-blue cord in graduated sizes. One set of beads was mostly pink; the other was mostly orange. He told us that when he was teaching, his students competed for one bead at a time, and top performers in class would end up with strands that were many feet long by the end of the year.

We hung one set of Murray beads from the rear-view mirror, to decorate the Squid Wagon, but I kept the other to wear as a necklace. Whenever I see them, it brings back that sunny day in Nebraska, listening to the wind blowing across the prairie and looking down at the tracks of the Oregon trail. George's handmade beads will always remind me of the importance of getting out of the car.

CHAPTER 21

A COUPLE OF SCAVENGER HUNTS
(INCLUDING MY BIGGEST FLOP)

The one and only time Barry and I drove through Maine, we sat in a cafe and had a conversation about what we wanted to do and see in this northernmost state. Should we go to the coast, or find the northern terminus of the Appalachian trail?

"There's a place in Maine I've always been curious about," I admitted. "Mooselookmeguntic Lake."

"Moose-what?" said Barry.

"It's the lake where my old friend Paul's family had a cabin. He talked about it a lot, and I've always wondered about it. I'd like to see the area."

Moose-what?

Twenty years earlier, Barry had heard all kinds of crazy stories about my former coworker, Paul, but he had never met him. We'd shared the most marvelous adventures, usually in the middle of the night, because we worked the evening shift. After Paul moved away, I often wondered what had become of him and what he was doing with his creativity and brilliance. I figured that New York City had swallowed him up, and that I'd never run into him again.

Once he understood the connection, Barry was curious about Mooselookmeguntic Lake, too. "We can go," he said, "but only on one condition: We have to try to find their cabin." We both thought spending a few days at this lake in Maine, asking after someone, was a good excuse to meet some local people, even if our search was totally in vain.

Barry and I were on a scavenger hunt. We had a mission, a quest, an excuse to poke our noses into places and ask questions. We had given ourselves an excuse to talk with strangers.

At 6:30 am, we started at the grocery store, the only place in town that was open. We struck up a conversation with the clerk, who was friendly, but didn't know anybody named Paul Chapman. After a few minutes, a local fellow came in, wearing plaid flannel. The clerk asked him if he knew the Chapman family. "Aye-yup," he answered. "Over behind the Fields' garages. And they're here" he said, significantly.

Barry and I looked at each other. Surely our scavenger hunt couldn't be this easy! Since it was still only 6:30, we drove to a park to eat breakfast. We were excited, but it would be polite to wait a few hours before knocking.

Around 9 o'clock, we drove up the narrow dirt track, where a BMW with New York license plates was parked. I recalled that Paul had always driven a BMW.

When we banged on the door, though, there was no answer. Maybe they had gone out for a walk? We got back in the Squid Wagon, and to my mortification, got completely stuck in their muddy driveway. For twenty minutes Barry and I did a lot of tire-spinning, pushing, and swearing. We finally made it out, leaving embarrassing evidence in the form of deep, ugly tire ruts.

We went back into the store again. A different fellow was behind the counter, and he knew Paul. "He was just here a few weeks ago, with his girls," he said. Really? I didn't know my friend had children.

The clerk assured us there was somebody staying at the cabin right now, probably a relative. When I told him nobody had answered the door, he explained, "Summer folks sleep in." Thinking of the racket we'd made in their driveway, I was sceptical.

In the spirit of the scavenger hunt, we drove 20 miles to the next town, to copy the permanent address from the tax records. If there was nobody at the cabin, at least I could write to Paul at home.

At midday, we decided to give the cabin one last try. I wasn't quite ready to give up on my scavenger hunt.

This time, we parked in a safe spot, away from the mud. When I got out, I looked around more carefully. Through the trees, only its roofline visible, was another cabin that we'd overlooked. There seemed to be no way to get to the front door, so we picked our way through the woods, over a path-that-was-not-a-path.

Nestled so well into the trees as to be almost invisible was a pair of small cabins, joined by a sweeping deck over the lake. Earlier that morning, we'd been knocking at the wrong cabin.

A woman came to the door, her face curious but open. I was nervous, unsure how to explain myself. I uttered about ten words before Paul's sister Melanie threw her head back and just started laughing and laughing. Somehow, I'd made it into family legend as "Margaret from Ohio," and after almost 20 years, she and her mother, neither of whom I'd met, knew exactly who I was.

They invited us in for coffee, and for the longest time, Melanie and Anne and I just kept looking at each other and laughing out loud, as if fate had always meant for us to meet in this remote place, in these unlikely circumstances.

We talked for hours, getting to know each other. Paul was the connection, but not the only topic of conversation. Anne, who was battling cancer in her 80's, had been a police reporter, socialist activist, and ad agency executive. Her life took her from Saskatchewan

*Nestled so well into the trees as to be almost invisible
was a pair of small cabins.*

to Ohio to New York, which is the place she liked best. She lost her
husband, whom they called "Big" Paul, just seven years prior.

They told us all about the cabin, which they'd owned for over 30
years. It was built in the 1800's, and in Maine style, they called it a
"camp." Only recently, they found out from a historian that the camp
was originally known as "The Crow's Nest." Melanie was ambivalent

about having a name for the place and thought it pretentious. But she said she couldn't argue with a name that went back a hundred years.

They both lived in New York, where Melanie was taking care of her mother full-time. She was lively and energetic, full of stories about friends, books, movies, music, and things they had done at the cabin. As a lifelong New Yorker, she had a funny story from every time she had been mugged, which was often.

Eventually, Melanie called Paul on her cell phone, and he and I talked for the first time in almost 20 years.

It was an awkward conversation; he sounded shocked to hear from me on his sister's phone. Meanwhile, Barry and the other two were having a grand time, and peals of laughter rang through the camp. We brought our cat in from the van, and she eagerly explored the interior of the cabin.

Barry and I spent the day with Anne and Melanie, swimming from their private beach, admiring their sailboat and canoe, and eating a delicious dinner that ended with flaming Bananas Foster. All day long, the four of us were always talking, laughing, layering our stories and experiences on top of each others'. That night, we slept in the Squid Wagon in their woods. The moon's reflection glittered over the black surface of the lake, and we awakened to a misty fog and chattering chipmunks.

When we started out on that cool Maine morning, all I had were the name of a lake, Mooselookmeguntic, and the name of a family. I thought the chances of finding the place were slim, and that at most, we might peer into the windows of an empty cabin I'd once heard stories about. I figured the scavenger hunt itself would be the most interesting part, an excuse to talk with some local folks.

Instead, we had a completely unforgettable day with Paul's family. With her cancer fairly advanced, I suspect that Anne passed away fairly

Dinner ended with flaming Bananas Foster.

soon after we met her. I never heard much from Paul after that, just one or two emails, and then we drifted apart again. The scavenger hunt wasn't really about finding my old friend, who preferred to stay lost. That just gave us an excuse to enjoy a magical day with two fascinating women on the shores of Mooselookmeguntic lake in Maine.

A number of years later, in Florida, we met a couple of "Mainers" from a lake near Mooselookmeguntic. Over breakfast, we shared with them the story of our successful scavenger hunt.

To our surprise, they were absolutely and completely shocked, asking us for more details in disbelief. It was as though they were trying to disprove the story.

As lifelong Maine residents, they explained that our experience went completely against Maine's close-mouthed, insular culture. People in Maine would never give out information to strangers like us.

The first clerk in the store, the one who said he didn't know any Chapmans? Sure, he knew them. He was lying to protect their privacy, they said.

The second clerk, who told us they were in the cabin, and we should go back and knock on the door? They suggested that he must have had a grudge against the Chapmans!

Not all of my scavenger hunts have the superb results of Mooselookmeguntic lake. My search for the Butter Divide was actually one of my biggest flops.

Driving across the country by myself, before I stopped to see Shirley in Spokane, I was terrified of being lonely. I decided that I should conduct a scavenger hunt of epic nationwide proportions. Then I'd have an excuse to talk with people in every town. That's why I decided to search for the Butter Divide, that mythical line, somewhere in the Midwest, where butter quarters are long and skinny to the east, and short and fat to the west.

There's a fine line between insanity and hilarity, and I am often on it.

From the beginning, when I mentioned the Butter Divide to people, they would either move away, as though I was nuts, or they would laugh. There's a fine line between insanity and hilarity, and I am often on it.

Those who don't think I'm nuts have hypothesized that the Butter Divide may coincide with the continental divide. Or it may follow the Mississippi River. Or that it doesn't exist, and butter shapes are completely random. So when I set out to drive from Seattle to North Carolina, I decided that my scavenger hunt would be to find the Butter Divide and follow it.

My first stop in the Hunt for the Butter Divide was in the small town of Cashmere, Washington. I went into the Hometown Market, where the butter looked just like the butter I'd left in Seattle, Darigold brand. Staring at the dairy case, I realized that I'd taken on an awfully big project, with no thoughts about how to do it. Should I take measurements and put them into a spreadsheet? Should I actu-

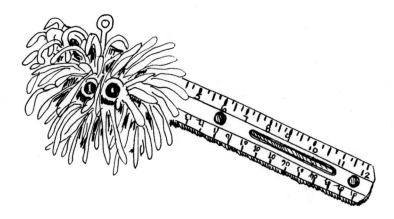

"You can get anything you need at Doan's."

ally be collecting data, or should I be interviewing people? Should I do both?

I decided to do both.

Still, I was woefully unprepared to seek the butter divide. Although I had the infamous orange satin evening gown in the car on that trip, I had forgotten to pack a ruler. How else would I take measurements and gather butter-stick dimensional data?

I walked up and down the aisles of the tiny grocery, but I didn't see any rulers. Finally, I went up to the cash register. The cashier was a woman with a movie-star black pageboy. When I told her that I was driving across the country and measuring butter, she threw her head back and laughed.

"Is somebody paying you to drive across the country and measure butter?" she asked, incredulous. I told her that not only was I not being paid, I was so scatterbrained I'd forgotten to bring a ruler. Did she know where I could buy one?

She sent me over to Doan's Pharmacy. It never ceases to amaze me what you can buy in a small town. At Doan's, I could buy an automated lift chair, a pack of playing cards, or a prickly squeezy toy. I also had my choice of several rulers — either a wooden one with a metal edge, or a plastic one that came in a rainbow of colors. Both were 12 inches long and cost 49 cents. "You can get anything you need at Doan's," the silver-haired cashier told me.

Watched her gently directing a developmentally disabled employee who was pricing merchandise, I agreed. The young woman was getting much more than a paycheck at Doan's.

I walked back to the grocery store with my new ruler and measured the butter boxes, and, just for kicks, the margarine boxes. I even took some pictures of the dairy case and the front of the store, so I'd have more data to put in my spreadsheet.

The movie-star cashier was busy when I was done, so I just waved my ruler at her and gave her a thumbs-up. She grinned back at me, causing the man who was talking to her to turn and stare curiously. Most people don't walk around grocery stores with rulers and cameras. Just those of us on the fine line between insanity and hilarity.

To my immense disappointment, I discovered over the next few weeks that the woman with the black pageboy was an anomaly. Nobody gave a hoot about the shape of butter quarters, especially grocery store checkers. They were either too busy to talk or too dis-

Unlike the Continental Divide, there's no sign
marking the Butter Divide.

interested to hold a conversation with a customer. Most of them seemed either bored or boring.

I did finally find the northern Butter Divide, just west of Bowman, North Dakota. I discovered this when I stopped to buy chocolate milk at the Super Valu grocery store.

At the checkstand, I excitedly told the checker that I had been traveling across the country, trying to figure out where the butter shape changed, and that *this was it.* "This is the Butter Divide," I said. "Bowman."

The woman ahead of me, who had just paid for her groceries, listened in and said, petulantly, "Is someone going to help me carry these out?"

"I will," said another checker. She glared at my checker, then pushed the old lady's cart out the front door.

"A dollar thirty-two," said my checker, snapping her gum.

It was so anticlimactic that I decided to continue driving east, rather than turning south to follow the Butter Divide. From the point of view of finding what I was looking for, it was a successful scavenger hunt. But it hadn't brought me the conversations I was hoping for. I hadn't had a single scintillating conversation about butter.

I'd had plenty of wonderful encounters, but none of them came about because of my research into the shape of butter sticks. That part was a total flop.

CHAPTER 22

MEPS' THEORY OF TRAVEL RELATIVITY

When I was a little girl, traveling across the USA in the back seat of my parents' Pontiac, I was fascinated by relativity as I understood it. We'd be driving down the freeway at 60 miles per hour, and sometimes, when we were in the left lane, a big semi-truck would be in the right lane, also going 60 mph. Since the truck driver and I were not actually traveling at a different speed, relative to each other, I had plenty of time to make eye contact and wave. I'd even have time to pick up one of the many teddy bears who rode with me, and he would wave a paw at the truck driver as well.

Based on this simplified theory of travel relativity, when I am traveling at the same speed as another person, on a bus, train, or airplane, we are actually not moving at all in relation to each other. Time spent this way may expand or contract, depending on how interesting the other person is.

In other words, time flies when you're having fun.

My teddy bear would wave a paw at the truck driver.

Barry and I once left our sailboat in a marina in a fairly remote marina in Port Angeles, Washington, and needed to get back to Seattle without a car. With a little research, we discovered that the 85-mile trip could be undertaken for less than ten dollars, if we were willing to ride four different buses and a ferry. By traveling most of the day, we could save a couple of hundred dollars in cab fare.

When we got off the first bus and were waiting for the second one, I noticed that we were not the only ones with luggage. A young man with very short hair was also waiting for the next bus, and his large green duffel bag rested at my feet on the sidewalk.

I poked Barry with my elbow and pointed, discretely, at the bag. In a mesh pocket on the side was an item clearly labeled "Fake Nose."

Barry and I were both stricken with the giggles at this, and it seemed unfair not to share the source of our mirth. I caught the young man's eye and pointed to his bag.

"Excuse me, I'm not trying to be, er, nosey…" (Barry snorted loudly at this) "…but may I ask why you are traveling with *that*?"

The young man looked at me, and then down at his duffel bag. Slowly, the joke took hold, and he joined our giggles.

It turned out that part of the packaging was obscured — the last word. It was actually a "Fake Nose Ring," and he had plans to surprise his friends by wearing it when he returned to Australia in a few months. "It will freak them out," he explained, with a grin.

Over the next few hours, with us as a captive audience, Tim shared one of the most interesting stories I've ever heard on a bus.

"May I ask why you are traveling with that*?"*

He was 19 years old and had been raised on a large pig farm in rural Australia. He was very proud of his farming background.

Tim's parents had one big regret. His father, too, had grown up on the farm. He married his high school sweetheart, worked the farm with his father, and grew a very large and successful business, with pigs, equipment, and employees. But Tim's parents had never had a chance to travel, and they could never take time off from the all-consuming pig farm.

Tim's parents still dreamed of being able to see the world before they were too old. So, after grooming their son to take over the family business, they sent him on a year-long round-the-world adventure, exploring the world and visiting pig farming operations along the way in the USA, Canada, Europe, and South America. The plan was for Tim to return and become a partner in the family business, at the ripe old age of 20. Then, while he was running the large operation, his parents could finally do the traveling they'd always wanted.

As the buses lumbered for hours along the 2-lane roads of the Olympic peninsula, with lush evergreen forests on one side and the blue, sparkling waters of Puget Sound on the other, time contracted and flew by. I felt like I was in a time warp, hearing stories about pig farming half a world away.

Time warp is a good way to describe the transition from our bear-free canoe trip on the Yukon River to the bus that took us to Dawson City. Barry and I had been alone in the wilderness for nine days, with no one to talk with but each other. It felt strange and sad to haul our canoe out of the river for the last time and pack up our backpacks.

We walked about a half mile up the road to a gas station-convenience store to wait for the bus. Carmacks was nothing but a crossroads in the middle of nowhere.

When the bus pulled into the parking lot, I was dismayed. It was an old blue-and-white school bus, not the kind of comfortable coach I was expecting. The driver, a slender gray-haired man in jeans and a

We were the brave adventurers on the bus.

Stetson hat, got out and placed a small plastic stepstool in front of the door, and a handful of people stepped off to stretch their legs.

Before meeting Mannfred and Peter and changing our plans in Skagway, we had originally planned to take this same bus all the way from Whitehorse to Dawson City. It would have been an all day trip. Yet after paddling for nine days, we had *still* only covered half the distance the bus traveled in a full day. Barry and I had four hours to ride on this contraption to get to Dawson City.

Carrying our backpacks, we waited until the others had reboarded the bus to take our seats. When we did, we were greeted by about a dozen faces, all of them full of curiosity. These folks had been on the bus since early morning. They were weary and a little bored with each other.

Barry and I were fresh blood, new people to talk with. They peppered us with questions about our trip. We were the brave adventurers on the bus.

The entire time we were on the bus, the conversations never stopped. Our bus-mates were from all over the world, so there were plenty of different viewpoints. The craziest passenger was a lady gold-miner from Australia who told everyone on the bus how the moon landing was a fake, staged event, and went on at great length about the conspiracy involved in keeping us all in the dark about that.

In our blue-and-white lumbering time warp, the hours flew by, unnoticed. Time contracted.

When we reached our destination, we all went our separate ways, to different lodgings. Barry and I pitched our tent in the local campground, literally on a street corner. With the exception of the crazy gold miner, the others had places reserved at various comfortable bed-and-breakfast establishments. None of us carried a cell phone in those days, so we didn't figure we'd see each other again.

We were wonderfully wrong about that.

The very next day, we ran into Corrie, our bus-mate from Toronto, on one of Dawson City's neatly graded but unpaved streets. On a whim, the three of us decided to poke our heads into the Westminster

At the Westminster Pub

Pub, a smoky but colorful local hangout. A group of folks had just started a jam session, taking turns on the guitar, piano, and fiddle, and we ended up staying for many hours and making plans to get together again the next day.

To anyone who saw the three of us, we probably looked like old friends who had a lot to talk about.

A few days later, Barry and I ran into Dawn and Vern, another couple from the bus. It was not only a holiday, Canada Day, but they were celebrating their 23rd wedding anniversary. As the four of us walked through town, we chanced upon Jim and Heidi, our British bus companions, and the six of us spent part of the day together. We all enjoyed making a big fuss over Dawn and Vern's anniversary.

To anyone who saw the six of us, we looked like old friends who had a lot to talk about.

We'd known each other for all of five days, but Travel Relativity made it seem like forever.

When I lived in Seattle, I knew two women who married their bus drivers, a little-known perk of driving a bus in that friendly city. Travel relativity doesn't just apply to long-distance travelers. It can happen to people who ride the same city bus each day.

One winter, I rode a commuter bus that originated in Stanwood, Washington. The weather was cold, damp, and dark. At the park-and-ride station, a single streetlight did little to dispel the gloom, and across the road, there was only a bleak, empty farmer's field.

I huddled at the bus shelter at 6:25 am, my teeth chattering from the unstoppable wind. I wished I had a car to wait in, like that other lady. She was sitting in the driver's seat, using the rear-view mirror to apply her makeup.

When she got out and joined me, she was friendly and chatty. "I hope the river doesn't flood today!" she said, cheerfully.

On the other side of the bleak farm field was the Stillaguamish river, nicknamed the Stilly. I knew there was a flood watch in effect, but I didn't realize it applied to the bus stop.

"At least, I hope I don't come back and find my car under water," she added.

I'd originally been a bit jealous when I noticed her sitting in her warm, toasty car. But now I felt a bit smug — my car was safely back at the house, out of reach of floodwaters. I'd heard that cars in this lot were often broken into, but I didn't realize they might flood as well. I began to wonder about this woman, whose choice to ride the bus meant not only hassle, but serious risk to her personal property.

For the next few months, I saw her whenever I rode the bus. She was always the first person to board, and she always sat in the front row, saving a seat for a woman who got on at the next stop. The two of them sat in those same seats every single day.

I took a month off, and when I returned, the days had lengthened. It was light enough that I could actually see her, a middle-aged lady, nicely dressed in a leather coat and low-heeled pumps.

"Hello!" she said. "You haven't been riding the bus lately."

I was surprised that she remembered me. "I went down to stay in Seattle," I told her. "It was nice to have a short commute for a while."

"Oh, I know what you mean," she replied, enthusiastically. "I used to live down there, and I really loved it, being right in town, where you can get to everything."

I wondered, out loud, how she ended up out here at the end of the bus line, with a daily commute that involved four hours on the bus. She told me that she and her husband had moved further away from town to raise their kids in the suburbs, then took an offer they couldn't refuse to buy his parents' house. Now they were stuck at the end of the bus line. Even though his parents no longer lived in the house, they were still emotionally attached to it.

"They'd be so mad if we sold the house, we can't move," she said. Living in that house, with a four-hour commute every day, was something she did to keep peace in her husband's family.

Yet it wasn't a sacrifice; she actually didn't mind the commute. The time spent on the bus gave her something most people don't have: Nearly four hours a day with her best friend.

Like the women who married their bus drivers, the two had met on the bus, many years earlier.

From my seat in the back, I watched them greet each other warmly, sharing the news of the day before turning to their respective magazines. Their entire friendship happened in those hours on the bus. Travel relativity gave them enough time to enjoy each others' company, and that made the lengthy commute more than worthwhile.

Trains are even more amazing than buses for exploring the theory of travel relativity. Trains are self-contained, and you can literally be on them for days with the same people, which makes it possible for relationships, and in our case, a reputation to develop.

Barry and I are not usually first-class travelers, but we had gotten two free first-class tickets from Seattle to Los Angeles aboard Amtrak's Coast Starlight. We had a roomette, a tiny private compartment with two seats that converted to a bunk bed. We'd been on the train for a couple of hours, playing with the convertible seats, reading the route literature, and watching out the window, when a polite, uniformed steward tapped on our door with a notepad in her hand. "Which seating would you prefer for lunch?" she asked.

Our first-class tickets included three meals a day in the dining car, plus a wine-and-cheese happy hour in the first class lounge car. We'd never experienced that kind of luxury, even if it was a sort of worn, faded luxury.

Because space in the dining car was limited, we had to sign up in advance for a time slot. The small booths seated four, so each meal was eaten facing another couple. We looked forward to talking with a different pair of strangers at every meal.

Barry and I have a little superstition on trains, a ritual. Every time a train enters a tunnel, we kiss. On that trip, we didn't think it was noteworthy, until the meal we shared with the Grumpy Couple.

They were an older couple, fractious with each other, cynical and sarcastic with us. They griped and complained about *everything*, from the food to the accommodations to the employees to the view. Seated directly across from them, it was impossible to ignore them, and extremely awkward to interact with them.

Suddenly, the windows went dark as the train entered a tunnel, and Barry and I turned and kissed each other. The woman made a snide remark about public displays of affection, and I apologized, explaining that we always kissed in tunnels. Our food came, and the four of us began to eat in silence.

What we didn't realize was that we were entering the most mountainous terrain of the trip. For over an hour, the train went into and out of tunnels constantly. Every few minutes, Barry and I had to quickly chew, swallow, and kiss. There was so much kissing to do, it was difficult to coordinate it with our breathing!

It became so ludicrous that we couldn't stop giggling, and the next thing we knew, the couple across from us was smiling. Then they were laughing, too. Once they thawed, the four of us enjoyed a pleasant conversation with our meal. The Grumpy Couple was actually smiling as they returned to their sleeper.

Then the train entered a tunnel...

The following day, we were seated across from yet another couple at breakfast. The terrain was flat, and the train hadn't gone through any tunnels for hours. As we waited for our food, the man across from us said he'd heard an interesting story. He had heard there was a couple on the train who kissed every single time the train went into a tunnel.

Barry and I burst out laughing and admitted that was us.

"Oh my God, that's *you?*" the man exclaimed. "You're famous! Everybody on the train knows about the Kissing Couple. We just didn't know it was you!"

It turned out that the Grumpy Couple had told everyone they met about the Kissing Couple. Word had spread throughout the train, but nobody knew who it was. Without knowing it, Barry and I had gotten a reputation, albeit one that only lasted as far as Los Angeles.

Travel relativity applies to planes, too.

When I arrived at the gate for my Charlotte flight to Seattle, most of the seats in the waiting area were taken. The other travelers avoided my eyes as I scanned the area, looking for a place to sit. I found a spot between a woman engrossed in a novel and a teenager engrossed in a cell phone. "But I texted her, and she never texted me back!" she complained, loudly, into the phone. Even my earphones couldn't drown out her grating, nasal voice.

Over the PA system, the gate crew announced that our flight would be completely full.

I boarded the plane and located my row. The man sitting in the aisle seat unbuckled his seat belt and stood to let me past, and I settled into the window seat, leaving one empty seat between us. There's a ritual we perform in these situations — buses, trains, planes, anyplace where we're going to be seated near (sometimes even touching) a total stranger for hours. First, there is an initial interaction, when we size each other up, making assumptions based on the other person's age, size, ethnicity, belongings, and behavior. Our assump-

Every seat on the plane was full, except one.

tions are turned into judgments, leading to an initial reaction: Positive, negative, or, very rarely, neutral.

Once we get settled, there's a second round of information-gathering. Based on our judgments, we might try to make eye contact. We might try *not* to make eye contact, but notice that the other person is trying. We also might make a comment to see how it's received — does the other person pick up the conversational ball, or let it drop?

After the man in the aisle seat and I were both settled, we made eye contact, and we smiled at each other. This led to a few comments, and the next thing we knew, we were so engrossed in our conversation that we didn't notice that the rest of the passengers were aboard until we heard the telltale clunk of the doors closing.

Then I craned my neck in amazement and looked around. Every seat on the plane *was* full, except for one — the seat between me and my row-mate. We tucked our bags under the spare seat and luxuriated (OK, that's an overstatement for coach class) in the extra space.

There's an interesting thing that sometimes happens at this point, when I have established that a stranger next to me is friendly. I take advantage of the fact that they are a stranger, and I'll probably never see them again, and I find myself sharing deeper feelings. The next thing I know, we are both talking about our hopes, our fears, our dreams, and all manner of vulnerable things that we don't normally share with our day-to-day friends.

Later, I may not remember their name, or what they looked like, but I will always remember the hopes and dreams and fears they shared with me. It's as if they've given me a special snow-globe. It's a precious memory that I can hold and look at every once in a while, and when I shake it, I get a glimpse into another person's life.

The man on the plane, whose name was Craig, was the father of five and the owner of a large construction business in the Seattle area. On a moment's notice, he'd left his family and business to help his brother, who'd just undergone three emergency surgeries. "He's going to be OK now," he said, the relief showing on his face.

I was on my own errand of mercy, but I was at the beginning, not the end, so I didn't know how it would turn out. I was flying to help a friend who was about to undergo a stem cell transplant, a difficult and dangerous treatment for cancer. Craig listened to my concerns knowingly.

As caregivers, he and I had a unique shared perspective. We both recognized that we were lucky people, because we had the health and resources to help others through difficult times.

As we compared our situations, we joked that the extra space of the empty seat between us was our reward for good deeds.

We began to explore all kinds of surprising topics. He shared his feelings about raising children, and how important wrestling was to his family. He told me how a life-and-death situation while boar-hunting in Hawaii made him address his beliefs about masculinity and pride. Blood-lust had caused him to do some things that went beyond foolish to stupid, things he wasn't proud to admit.

Who better to admit those things to, than a kind and compassionate stranger?

Safe in our snow-globe, the hours compressed to minutes. Craig and I didn't talk as if we were strangers. Today, if I passed him on the street, I don't think I'd recognize his face. I'd only know him if I got into a conversation with him again.

CHAPTER 23

I SHOULD HAVE BOUGHT A LOTTERY TICKET

I am completely fascinated with coincidences and serendipity. For instance, an hour after meeting the truck driver named Fred Sanford in a parking lot in Pennsylvania, I drove past an antique shop in Maryland called Sanford & Sons. If I hadn't talked with Fred, I wouldn't have even noticed their sign.

The most amazing coincidences are the ones that bring me together with just the right person at the right time, the one who has the answers I need. Everything I have done, and everything they have done, conspires to put us together in this moment. Given that, every encounter with a stranger is a miracle.

While I was in Summit, South Dakota, charming the folks at the bar and the cafe, a second story began to develop. I didn't have a phone, so once a day I would drive out to the truck stop by the interstate, a place with minimal soul and many gas pumps called The Coffee Cup. I'd get a large, cheap, highly caffeinated cup of coffee and sit at one of the worn formica-topped tables to check my email.

*The Coffee Cup had minimal soul
and many gas pumps.*

In one message, I mentioned to my friend Tina, the daughter of the infamous Shirley of Spokane, that I was in a small town in South Dakota. She wrote back, telling me that Shirley had grown up in Watertown, South Dakota and still had a brother who lived there.

What a coincidence — Watertown, population 20,000, was the next town over from Summit!

I decided to drive down there and look up Shirley's brother, who owned a large automotive body shop.

I had no trouble finding Crocker's Collision Center, and soon I was seated in Ray's nicely-furnished office, telling him about my recent visit with his sister, whom he hadn't seen in a few years.

"But what are you doing *here*?" he asked me, puzzled. I explained how I'd been looking for a quiet place to stay and write, and had accidentally landed in Summit.

"Really?" he said. "My father grew up in Summit."

It was my turn to be surprised. A few weeks after meeting Shirley in Spokane, I randomly ended up in Summit, population 267. Then her brother told me their father was from there!

When I went back to Summit that evening, I asked the folks in the bar if anyone knew of the Crocker family, but they all said no. The next day, I stopped into the hardware store and asked Mitzi, the woman with the Kitty Cat snowmobiles, whether she knew any Crockers. "No, but wait a minute," she said.

Mitzi rummaged under the counter and came up with a dusty box. "This is stuff from our centennial," she told me. Inside the box were a couple of books that had been compiled with lists and maps of everyone who had lived in Summit for the first hundred years. "You can borrow these and see if there's anything about your friends," she said. I picked up a beer can cozy, with an illustration of Summit's main street and the words SUMMIT CENTENNIAL across the top. At the bottom were the dates, July 3–5, 1992. "You can keep that," said Mitzi. Seventeen years after the centennial, she still had a pile of them.

I spent a couple of days going through the history books, and finally found an entry for E.G. Crocker, "farmer and stockraiser," dated 1885. I had been super-excited for Tina when she found her birth mother. Now I couldn't wait to tell her that I'd stumbled upon information on her ancestors in this unlikely place.

On my last day in Summit, I packed the car and drove to the hardware store on my way out of town. Mitzi wasn't at the store, but her husband, Royce, was. I loved the place; it was the kind of old-fashioned hardware store where nobody was in a hurry, and men sat around, shooting the breeze. Royce had company; a couple of men I didn't know were sitting and talking with him, and they fell silent when I came in.

I put the books on the counter and told Royce why I was returning them.

"Did you find what you were looking for?" he asked.

"Yes, I was looking for the Crocker family, and they're in here," I said. "But I haven't found any Crockers still living in town…"

I was interrupted by a voice from behind me. "Did you say Crocker?"

I turned around; one of the men sitting across from the sales counter was standing up. And up, and up, and up — a giant of a man, well over 6½ feet tall, stuck out his hand, and I shook it.

"My grandmother was a Crocker," he said. "My name is Miter."

Miter

I couldn't believe the coincidence. I finally met the mysterious Miter, and he was related to Shirley and Tina!

"Do you want to see the old farmhouse where the Crockers lived?" he offered. "I can take you out there."

"Sure," I said. When I opened the door of his big red pickup, I found a rather large gun in the passenger seat. "Oh, sorry — I'll move that," said Miter, scooting it over to the middle of the cab, between us. I paused, wondering whether I was crazy to climb into a vehicle with a giant, gun-toting stranger. Then I decided he wasn't all that strange, and I got into the truck.

I don't know why I thought the drive would be short, like five minutes, but I was wrong. We drove for about 30 minutes on ruler-straight but unpaved roads just to get to the family farm. Then we drove over to the cemetery where all the Crockers were buried. Then to a second farm, one owned by another generation of Crockers. We talked nonstop, about family and generosity and creativity and traveling.

Miter was so interesting, I could have talked to him all day. I understood why Ernie and Lynn had wanted me to meet him.

When Miter returned me to my little car, parked in front of the hardware store, I was beaming, despite the dreary drizzle. The time we spent together was full of satisfying conversation, and unlike anything I'd experienced in my six-day stay in Summit.

When it comes to coincidences, the weirdest ones are when the strangers I run into turn out not to be strangers at all.

One day in February, *Flutterby* was rocking and rolling at anchor in Factory Creek, across from Beaufort, South Carolina. We were hunkered down, waiting out the howling winds left over from a major storm system that had wrecked havoc across the southern United States, bringing tornadoes, death, and destruction. At dusk, Barry went up on deck to check on the situation, and to my surprise, I heard him talking to someone.

He came back down, shaking his head. "A nice lady on the dock invited us over for a glass of wine," he said.

"Wow. It looks so close, but it's a million miles away, isn't it?" I replied.

We were barely 100 feet from a private dock in front of a condo building, but in the high winds, it was nearly impossible to launch our tiny rowing dinghy, *Flutterwent.*

The next day, the winds calmed a little, and we were able to row ashore for errands. A new GPS set us back $1000, and combined with a difficult row against a 2-knot current, we were tired and grumpy.

When we got back to *Flutterby* that evening, we wearily hauled the dinghy up on deck and tied it down. My mind was set on an early bedtime and a pre-dawn departure.

On the dock in front of the condos, a man called to get my attention. "Would you like to come over for a glass of wine?" he shouted.

If he'd called out 10 minutes earlier, I might have said yes. But I shook my head. "No thank you," I answered. I pointed to the dinghy I'd just hauled up on deck and shrugged.

He persisted, having noticed our home port. "Our daughter lives in Seattle."

"Oh, where?"

"On Capitol Hill."

Shouting back and forth over the loud wind made for a very difficult conversation. However, he told me where his daughter lived; to my surprise, it was only a few blocks from the house Barry and I owned for 10 years.

"I'm not originally from Seattle!" I shouted. I told him that my parents had built a house on nearby Harbor Island.

"What's your Dad's name?" he asked.

"Schulte."

He threw his head back, laughing. "I WAS AT YOUR WEDDING!"

"I WAS AT YOUR WEDDING!"

I peered closely at the white-haired gentleman on the dock, whom I hadn't seen in over 20 years. Then I stuck my head down the companionway. "Barry! We have to launch the dinghy again! That's Tom Mikell on the dock!"

We launched the dinghy and rowed the short distance. Tom was waiting for us with a glass of wine in a condo on the ground floor, *Flutterby's* red hull and blue masts perfectly framed in the french doors of the living room.

The three of us sat down and started getting caught up. "Wait 'til my wife comes back from yoga. She's going to be amazed. She was disappointed when you wouldn't come over yesterday."

Mary Ann came back a little while later, and Tom met her at the door. "We have guests, honey. Remember those folks on the sailboat?"

"Great! You got them to come over!" She greeted us with a big smile and a hug, and Tom teased her about his ability to lure us over when she could not. Then he burst out, "Guess who was at their wedding!" She shook her head, "Who?"

Tom pointed to himself.

All three of us grinned at her. She stared at us in disbelief, then checked the wine bottle. "What have you been drinking?"

"It was twenty years ago," I chimed in.

With all three of us talking at once, we explained the strange coincidence, the fact that Tom had known my parents very well, that we had gotten married at my parents' house in a memorable and unusual ceremony. "Do you remember that there was a sailboat on top of the cake?" I said to Tom. Back then, we owned a 14-foot daysailer and dreamed of someday cruising on a "big" boat.

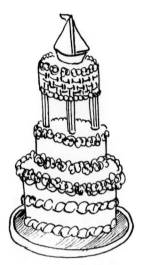

Tom and Mary Ann had been married for just about a year. A wonderfully-matched couple, both of them were excellent story-tellers who shared a lively sense of humor.

"I met your Mom and Dad at a party on Harbor Island," said Tom. He was an attorney who represented the Harbor Island Owners' Association, an organization my Dad practically ran for a while. "When I got there, everybody was drinking and carrying on, and your Mom had this party game, where she was studying peoples' handwriting."

There was a sailboat on top of the cake.

I cracked up laughing. Mom's ability and belief in handwriting analysis were legendary in my family. Any time my siblings or I brought home a new boy- or girlfriend, Mom demanded a sample of their handwriting to analyze and make sure they were a good person. Barry evaded her scrutiny only because handwriting analysis required cursive writing, and he refused, stubbornly printing everything.

"So your Mom studies this sample of my handwriting," continued Tom, "and with everybody at the party watching, she looks at me and says, 'Hmm, dishonest...' and everyone at the party starts laughing their heads off! 'See these loops here, and the way the i's are dotted...dishonest, very dishonest. Must be a lawyer.' I must admit, I was not pleased," said Tom. He scowled playfully.

Luckily, Tom forgave my mother and enjoyed many good times with both my parents. He described a time when Harbor Island was a tight-knit community of young, vibrant retirees who hung out together on the beach, went boating, and had a lot of parties.

"Remember the whale?" he said.

That was another legendary story — in 1987, a 65-foot whale beached herself on Harbor Island, which is really just an overgrown sandbar. My family was walking on the beach that day and were the first people to discover the giant, dying creature. The whale was euthanized after a couple of days, but then there was the problem of

One of Tom's more interesting legal cases

what to do with a rotting 65-foot whale — one of Tom's more interesting legal cases.

A group of experts cut the whale up into pieces with chainsaws, and the island residents hired a man with a bulldozer to bury them. But Mother Nature had other ideas, and a couple of weeks later, rotting whale pieces started popping up out of the sand. The smell was unbearable.

"I guess they just buried it deeper," said Tom.

"I heard they had to pour a *lot* of concrete on top," I said. Neither of us had heard of whale problems on the island after that.

I had another encounter, a few years earlier, that was even more astonishing than anchoring in front of Tom's house. Two minutes one way or the other, and it would never have happened.

I'd just driven alone across Montana on mind-numbingly boring two-lane roads. As much as I loved the beautiful scenery, I struggled with loneliness, and I was desperate to get out of Montana and see if I could find people to talk with in North or South Dakota. I hadn't yet found the Butter Divide, or the bar in Summit.

I spent my last night in Montana in a squeaky-clean but depressing motel on the edge of Miles City, a place so hard-up for business that they could only charge $20 for a room. When I got up in the morning, I asked the owner if she could recommend a restaurant for breakfast. The place she told me about was back in Miles City, and

I reluctantly backtracked the few miles to the west. I didn't want to spend any more time in Montana than I had to.

In hindsight, I recognize that everything I did that morning contributed to the coincidence. What time I woke up, how long I stayed in the shower, where I went for breakfast — even how long it took for them to take my order and cook my breakfast — everything put me in the right place at the right time.

I had left the restaurant and driven for about a half hour down a two-lane road when I saw a sign that said "Parking area ahead." I was going to ignore it, but I noticed that it had a bathroom, so I suddenly put on the brakes, turned in, and parked. Finding a bathroom in this part of Montana was a little miracle; they were rare as hen's teeth on the two-lane roads. I'd watered a fair amount of sagebrush in this stretch of the trip.

When I turned off the car and stepped out, the silence was deafening. There was no sound but the wind and some crickets. From where I stood, there wasn't another human being, another car, a house, or even a cow to be seen.

I carefully stayed on the sidewalk going to the toilet, recalling signs in other Montana rest areas that said, "Rattlesnakes have been observed. Please stay on sidewalks."

I nervously checked the toilet for snakes, but the coast was clear. It was a very clean and bright pit toilet.

So hard-up for business that they could only charge $20 for a room

When I came out, another car had pulled up and parked. A tall, broad-shouldered man was striding towards the bathroom, ignoring the paved path. I thought to myself, "That guy's not afraid of rattlesnakes." I noticed that there was a woman with him, a tiny lady who was just getting out of the car.

That's when I realized, with a shock, that *I knew them*.

That September 23, at 9:36 in the morning, my husband's only uncle and his wife had stopped to use the same bathroom I had.

As Johnny walked towards me, I just stood and stared at him. It became apparent that he was going to walk right past me, because he didn't recognize me. How could he, when I was completely out of context?

We were thousands of miles from any place I had ever called home. As far as Johnny knew, I should have been aboard my boat in North Carolina, or at his brother's house near Seattle, or any place in the world except State Route 12 in Montana.

"Excuse me, you're Johnny, aren't you?" I asked. Johnny stopped. "Yes, I am." "From Minnesota?" I asked. Now he was looking puzzled. Who was this strange woman?

"I'm Margaret," I said.

He just looked puzzled. "You know, Barry's wife?" There was a pause. Then recognition and amazement flashed across his face.

Johnny and Sooky's property in Montana

"Sooky, come over here!" he hollered to his wife, and she came over to see who he was talking to. We were all shocked at the miracle of our improbable meeting.

I had driven about 1,000 miles from Seattle, with plans to continue another 2,000 miles to North Carolina. Johnny and Sooky had driven 800 miles from Minneapolis to check on two pieces of property they owned in Montana. Although they had planned to stay for a few more days, Sooky woke up with such a bad case of poison ivy, they suddenly changed their plans and decided to drive straight to their doctor in Minnesota.

Now the three of us stood in the grass, the only humans for miles and miles. My terrible loneliness vanished, replaced with pure awe. *This* was serendipity.

"I wondered why you were staring at me," said Johnny, chuckling. He turned to his wife and said, "We should go buy a lottery ticket!"

CHAPTER 24

HOMEBODIES

A saleslady at a suburban Ohio furniture store said to me, suc-cinctly, "I wish I had *your* life."

She had just been telling me about her college-aged daughter, who was an award-winning published author at 21.

"I wish I had your daughter's life!" I responded.

People who stay home think that my life is fascinating, and their lives are boring. Their lives are not boring to *me*.

I go out of my way to meet strangers who don't travel. I want to know what their lives are like. What's it like to be a human being in a small town in West Virginia, a Newfoundland fishing village, or a ranch in Texas? What's it like to sell furniture every day?

W hen I lived in rural North Carolina, I met a woman who lived on a farm and sold vegetables and fruits from an open-air roadside shack. She had never traveled further than a few hundred

What's it like to sell furniture every day?

Surrounded by strawberry fields

miles within the state, and she had never flown on an airplane in her entire life. Yet her ancestors had settled the land in the 1700's, and her life was full, with family, friends, and church connections.

What I loved about spending time with Belle was her enthusiasm and her upbeat attitude, her loyalty to her family, and her deep roots. She found my nomadic life fascinating and told me over and over how brave I was. "I can't believe you drove all the way across 'merica alone," she said, shaking her head. "I ain't never even drove my own car outside Carteret county!"

Because her horizon never changed, Belle didn't recognize the adventure in her own life. It was right in the produce stand, surrounded by strawberry fields. Over her lifetime, she had been visited by thousands of friends, neighbors, and strangers. Each car that pulled into the dirt parking lot brought her a new encounter, a new set of possibilities, without Belle having to leave home at all.

Like Belle, I once believed that living a "normal" life at home precluded any sort of noteworthy adventure. In 2001, Barry and I were between travels, working at eight-to-five office jobs in Seattle. We had all the headaches that went with the desk-jockey lifestyle — long commutes, not enough exercise, a house with a mortgage, a car that needed repairs. We had a few friends and a small sailboat, the *Northern Crow*, that allowed us to get away on weekends.

On Labor Day, we were motoring back to our marina, returning to our home and jobs after the long weekend. Suddenly, our engine died as we approached the Seattle Locks. We managed to drift to the side of the channel and tie up to a slimy, barnacle-encrusted wall.

While Barry had his head in the engine compartment, I scanned the empty faces on the passing powerboats, hoping to hail someone who could help. But no one would even meet my eye, causing me to grumble about the uselessness of boats that resembled giant Clorox bottles. Finally, I spied an intelligent-looking bearded fellow on a small, classic wooden Chris Craft. When I waved vigorously, he smiled and turned his boat in our direction. Little did I know how that wave was to impact my future.

I had the good fortune to choose, as our rescuer, none other than the infamous Captain Craig, the self-titled Scourge of Lake Union and Environs. After we had explained our problem, he offered to tow our boat back to the slip, a trip of about an hour. Once we had secured our lines, he cast a practiced eye on our boat and asked us, "What have you got to drink?"

I was embarrassed by the question, because we'd been dieting. "Uh, water," I stammered, "and a little soymilk, I think."

"That simply will not do!" boomed Captain Craig. "Sara, fix these folks a gin and tonic."

By the time we reached our marina, our dead engine seemed hilarious, and we were fast friends with Craig and Sara. We exchanged phone numbers and e-mail addresses, and the following spring, I got

Seven people scratching themselves, jumping up and down, and hooting like monkeys

a call. "Craig here," said the deep voice on the phone. "Would you like to go on my boat for the Opening Day Parade?"

The theme for the parade was "Jungle Party," and when we arrived aboard *Flagrante Delicto*, our host produced animal masks for us to wear. For about an hour, we milled around the bay with hundreds of other boats, waiting. A yacht club boat passed by, and a woman in a blue blazer and white pants called across the water, with a slight accent, "That's a nice boat! What does the name mean?" We all turned to stare at our skipper, to see how he would respond. Meanwhile, the lady's boat drifted farther away, and Craig had to shout. "IT MEANS 'CAUGHT IN THE ACT!'" She called back, puzzled, "OF WHAT?" We were rolling in laughter. "OF SEX!" he hollered, loudly, because they were quite far now. "Of SEX?" she repeated back, then realized what she'd shouted. She clapped her hands over her mouth, aghast, and quickly ducked out of sight into the boat's cabin, her face red.

We did not win a prize for our animal act, which consisted of seven people scratching themselves, jumping up and down, and hooting like monkeys. We should have won a prize for chutzpah, though.

Just as we passed in front of the parade judges, *Flagrante Delicto's* engine died. Our skipper dived into the cabin, where I thought he was rooting around for a spare part. Instead, he produced the most battered bugle I'd ever seen, then stood at the helm of his drifting boat and played the haunting notes of Taps. The incredulous crowd ate it up, hooting with laughter. Craig's version of the song had more cracked notes than I knew a bugle could produce.

The judges scowled. Evidently, this was the second year in a row that this had happened.

As we drifted, powerless and off key, we were blocking the parade route. A police boat came out and the officer grabbed our line and towed us out of the way. "Can you fix it?" he asked. "Sure, I can try," said Craig, looking as smart and efficient as that day I'd picked him out of the Clorox bottle lineup for a rescue. To my shock, the police officer took us to a navigational aid, the number 15 green can, and told us to tie up.

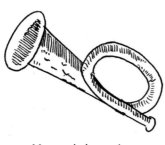

*More cracked notes than
I knew a bugle could produce*

The first thing I learned in a Coast Guard Auxiliary boating class was: Do not ever, ever, *ever* tie up to a navigation aid. But who could argue with a police officer? I looked nervously over at Craig, expecting him to dive into the engine, fix the problem, and untie the boat. To my surprise, he poured himself a drink. "I, for one, am not going to disturb the food," he said. It was true, the engine compartment was completely covered with salads, chips, cookies, dishes, and beverages. "Hey, look at that!" He distracted me by pointing at the next boat in the parade.

We did have the best seats in the house. We were literally across from the judges' boat, alone on our buoy, not jockeying for space or bumping into a bunch of other boats. My new friend Craig knew what he was doing: It didn't get any better than this.

At the end of the day, Craig hailed a friend — he knew dozens of people out on the water — who towed us back across the lake. Just outside his marina, he said, "Let's see how this works…" He turned the key, and to my shock, the engine started! Was it really a fuel starvation problem, as he claimed, or a ruse to get the best seat in the house for the Opening Day parade? I've been out on *Flagrante Delicto* dozens of times since then, and it has never happened again.

What has happened, over and over again, is that Captain Craig has introduced me to dozens of amazing people, both on *Flagrante Delicto* and ashore. Those people have introduced me to dozens and dozens more, until my circle includes hundreds of the most creative people in Seattle: Artists, musicians, engineers, software designers, sailors, dancers, doctors, and entrepreneurs. Meeting Craig on the water was a completely life-changing encounter with a stranger, and I was only five miles from home when it happened.

Captain Craig indirectly got us into adventures most eight-to-fivers never even dream of. That one encounter led me to Shirley in Spokane, Miter in Summit, and Carlos in Portugal. It was even on *Flagrante Delicto* that a new friend said, "Please come to Burning Man with us!"

I always fondly remembered the good times we had with Harley and Annabelle, the musicians we met in the state park in New Mexico, in the early 90's. In the days before email, though, it was easy to lose track of each other. I forgot their last name and the name of the town where they lived, but I never forgot their faces, their stories, or their music. I never forgot the colorful children's book that Annabelle wrote and illustrated, or her smiling comment, "It's such a beautiful day, even the birds are singing about it!"

Luckily, I remembered their distinctive first names. I also remembered that they were from a little town in Oklahoma, somewhere on the Texas border.

Fifteen years later, the world had changed. I had Google.

At the time, Barry and I were packing the contents of our apartment in Seattle, getting ready to put our belongings in storage and move across the country to *Flutterby* in North Carolina. The floor was littered with boxes and piles as I sat down at my computer.

I didn't say anything to Barry about my search. It was so unlikely, I felt silly as I typed three words: Harley Annabelle Oklahoma.

"Omigod!" I exclaimed.

My exclamation was enough for Barry to climb over the piles of stuff on the floor and peer curiously over my shoulder.

Thousands of links from all over the world had popped up about our old friends. Their Sandhills Curiosity Shop was located on Old Route 66 and was now known as the "Redneck Capital of the World." There were hundreds of pictures of Harley and Annabelle, in red-and-white striped overalls, holding guitars. There were videos of them playing "Get Your Kicks on Route 66."

The people we had met in a remote New Mexico campsite were famous.

I found an old picture, scanned it, and attached it to an email.

"Do you remember us?" I wrote. I told them we were going to be passing that way for the first time since we met them in 1993, and that we'd like to stop and see them.

My crazy Google search: Harley Annabelle Oklahoma

Sure enough, they wrote back with an enthusiastic invitation: "Yes, we do remember 'two gals walking by.' We're looking forward to seeing you after all these years and sharing our story with you."

Theirs is the story of two people who stayed home.

Harley had been a professional musician for years before we met them, playing on the country music circuit with a lot of big names. Eventually, he burned out. He got tired of life on the road and moved into some property that had belonged to his parents, in the dying town of Erick, Oklahoma. It was right at the Texas border on I-40.

Annabelle was visiting a relative in Erick when she walked into Harley's 100-year-old storefront. She'd been looking for guitar strings. Instead, she found Harley, and they fell in love.

But it wasn't easy to make a living in Erick, Oklahoma. Nobody ever came into the store, which was located directly on the old Route 66. The interstate had bypassed Erick.

In the early 1990's, the two spent their summers camping in New Mexico state parks and selling musical instruments and guitar strings at a flea market outside Santa Fe. That's when Barry and I met them.

A number of years later, in 1999, the two were sitting in that same storefront in Erick, Oklahoma, wondering how to pay their bills. They picked up their guitars and started jamming to take their minds off their financial woes. A man walking by stuck his head in the door and said, "Wow, you guys are great! I have a tour bus full of folks outside," he said. "We're driving the length of Route 66. Can I bring them inside for some music?"

The tourists, who were from the UK, trooped into the dim, cool shop, and Harley and Annabelle put on an impromptu show for them. At the end, they passed the hat, and from that moment on, their money troubles were over. The little storefront, which had been an unsuccessful health food store, an unsuccessful music store, and an unsuccessful antique store, became a hugely successful tourist attraction.

Harley and Annabelle were the new stars of Route 66.

Every day, travelers from all over the world stopped to see them, in tour buses, motorcycle rallies, and rental cars. Annabelle, an artist as well as a musician and writer, welcomed them with colorful handmade signs that featured prominently in the group photos. They welcomed the travelers with drinks and snacks, and then they put on an unforgettable show. Afterwards, they passed the hat.

A few weeks after my fateful Google search, Barry and I pulled up in front of the Sandhills Curiosity Shop. Harley and Annabelle recognized us immediately. I was quickly enveloped in a bone-crush-

Annabelle and Harley

ing hug from great big Harley. Annabelle's smile was just as gentle and kind, and her voice as soft, as I remembered.

I took in the visual overload of Route 66 memorabilia and collectables on the walls, tables, ceiling, and floor. To call it a shop was a misnomer, because even though it was completely full, from floor to ceiling, Harley and Annabelle didn't seem to have prices on anything.

There were hundreds of photos of tour groups, along with cards, gifts, and clippings they've received from all over the world. When we arrived, they were entertaining a couple from Holland, Ernst and Annette, who were driving the entire length of Route 66. There was a lot of silly banter, and Harley flirted outrageously with all three ladies. I laughed so hard, I got a cramp in my jaw. Harley gave me laugh-face.

Finally, they picked up their guitars. They called themselves "The Mediocre Music Makers," but that was a complete joke — there was nothing mediocre about these two. Annabelle's voice was more beautiful than I remembered as they played "What a difference a day makes." And when Harley started in on a guitar solo, I felt like I was a special guest in a Nashville recording studio. These two were *good*. Next, they played a song they wrote together that gave me goosebumps: "It's such a beautiful day, even the birds are singing about it." They finished up with their trademark, "Get your kicks on Route 66."

Harley and Annabelle gave us many gifts that day, from the hugs to the music to the kisses they blew as we drove away. The best gift of all was knowing that these two friends, who I'm proud to say I knew before they were famous, had so many friends and fans all around the world. While I was out traveling the world, they stayed home, in their Redneck Castle in tiny Erick, Oklahoma, where they were discovered by thousands of people who really loved and appreciated them.

Rediscovering Harley and Annabelle taught me that there's nothing wrong with staying home. With a joyful, open heart, it doesn't matter where you are. The world will come to you.

With a joyful, open heart, it doesn't matter where you are.

CHAPTER 25

KINDRED SPIRITS

When Donna said to me, in the diner in Pennsylvania, "You have friends everywhere you go," I was quick to protest. Oh, no, not me. I just have little chats with strangers.

But Donna was right about one thing: My address book is completely full of former strangers.

It's true that I enjoy talking to just about everyone I meet (Chicken Pox man was a noteworthy exception). But there are some who stand out, whose company is a special treat. Like George, the teacher with the beads on the Oregon trail, some people's conversation and company is so natural, they seem like friends immediately.

Those strangers go into my address book. I stay in touch, so I have friends everywhere I go.

Laundromats are grim places, usually poorly maintained and lacking soul. They always have a lot of misspelled signs that start with the word "Don't." They usually have at least one sign that says "Out of Order."

The last laundromat I was in, on a busy highway outside Charleston, South Carolina, had lots of spider webs up near the ceiling, full of dead bugs. There was a large expanse of flooded, stained floor.

I met one of my best friends in a place like this.

It seemed like a dreadfully unclean place to seek cleanliness for my clothing.

Despite that, I always have a moment of eager anticipation when I walk into a laundromat. I discovered a kindred spirit, one of my best friends, in a place just like this.

Barry and I were in Lunenburg, Nova Scotia, on the east coast of Canada, sorting our socks in a laundromat called "The Soap Bubble." On the counter, we'd set aside the notebook where we were compiling a grocery list.

A tall, lanky guy with a neatly trimmed beard came into the laundry. He was stuffing his clean clothes into a compact orange duffel bag when he glanced our way. "Cruising Notes," he read out loud from the cover of the notebook. "Are you cruisers?"

I looked down at the medium-sized notebook, one of a half-dozen I'd accidentally-on-purpose removed from the supply room at a former employer. At the time, Barry had complained, "I can't tell them apart!" so I decorated each one differently with markers, stickers, and ribbons. This one, as the man noticed, said "Cruising Notes" in inch-high letters, with pictures of waves and junk-rigged sailboats and globes. We were using it for shopping lists, notes, limericks, doodles — everything but the sailboat-cruising notes for which it was originally intended.

"Are you cruisers?"

Folks who cruise on sailboats usually have no trouble recognizing each other. They end up in the same anchorages, marinas, or waterfront pubs, and they know each other as much by the names of their boats as by their given names. They carry the same canvas tote bags and wear the same jackets, like a uniform.

However, at the time, Barry and I were boatless. That made it harder to find someone who spoke our language. We yearned to spend time with people who understood the call of the sea, whose native tongue was "boat."

In a very short time, in the Soap Bubble, we discovered that Kris was a sailboat cruiser, working on a circumnavigation of North and South America. He carried a South African passport, but his accent was that wonderful mix of sounds that indicated he had lived in many, many places. He told us he was "a professional foreigner."

At the time, he was staying in a boatyard, doing some work aboard a tall ship named *Larinda*. "Come on down and see her," he said. "Most people call her a junk rig, but you'll recognize it as a fully-battened lug rig."

That evening, Barry and I wandered down to the *Larinda* for a look. Although she was floating, she was a project boat more daunting than any I'd ever seen: All the furnishings were ripped out and the engine removed, with bare sections of ferrocement hull recently patched that were slowly being cured. Kris was especially proud of his ingenious system to keep the concrete damp as it cured, something involving a timer and some parts from a washing machine. It made wet, hissing noises in a dark corner of the cabin precisely every ten minutes.

Larinda, *in her glory days*

Looking around belowdecks, I was confused by what I saw. The boat looked ancient, like an old hulk that had been abandoned for decades. But she had only been launched six years prior, after 28 years of loving construction by the man who dreamed her into existence. The dark, stripped cabin, which looked like some sort of steerage quarters, had been full of varnished wood, shiny brass, and elegant upholstery.

The impact of Hurricane Isabel, which hit the Chesapeake in 2003, was so devastating to the United States that most Americans were unaware of the following storm, Hurricane Juan. Juan made unprecedented landfall at Halifax, Nova Scotia, a city so far north that they'd never been hit by a hurricane in recorded history.

Larinda was one of the victims. Holed by another boat in 100-mph winds, she sank right in the harbor. As if that wasn't tragic enough, it was directly under an untreated sewer outfall. There she sat, collecting poop, for three weeks before being salvaged.

When she was finally salvaged, she passed into the hands of a different owner — a professional who happened to be in the business of treating poop. By the time we saw the boat, she had been stripped, scrubbed, and sanitized. She still looked dreadful, but she was no longer full of bacteria and used condoms. She smelled of raw concrete, not raw sewage.

Our tour of the 80-foot vessel ended, appropriately, in the forward head, where I could make out signs of the boat's former grandeur. Over the bathtub, with its whimsical frog fixtures, the walls were covered with full-color hand-painted tile showing *Larinda* in her former glory, all her butterfly-like sails set. She had been a beauty, and she would be a beauty again.

Back in the dimly-lit galley, or what remained of it, our new friend broke out a bottle of Cuban rum he'd been saving, and we launched into a few hours of our favorite activity, "Sea Stories and Fairy Tales." * Our laughter was punctuated by the ten-minute rhythm of Kris' sprayer in the corner.

In the next few weeks, the three of us got together often for conversation and hijinks. At the pub, we shared cheap poutine, that uniquely Canadian concoction of french-fried potatoes covered with gooey gravy and melted cheese. We drove many miles out of town to a bluegrass concert that featured musicians of great enthusiasm but dubious ability. We shared a Thanksgiving dinner in which the main course — a stuffed squash, not a turkey — was carved and served with a hatchet.

One evening, Kris invited us to *Larinda* for dinner. He set up a propane camping stove on the bare counter, and he began frying some battered fish in a skillet.

---

* On a boat, it is important to know whether someone is telling you a sea story or a fairy tale. The difference is simple: Fairy tales always begin with "Once upon a time..." Sea stories are otherwise indistinguishable but always begin with "Now, this ain't no shit..."

*Forcing the pieces of fish
into the slots*

"Damn!" he swore. He clicked the lighter on the stove, but it was no use. He had run out of propane, and the fish sat forlornly in the skillet, only halfway cooked.

"That's all right, we have a camping stove out in the van," Barry told him. He ducked out to the Squid Wagon in the rain and didn't hear Kris say, "Why don't you just bring the fuel bottle?"

While he was gone, I explained to Kris that our stove wasn't propane, so we couldn't just swap out the bottle. He watched curiously as Barry set it up on the galley counter. It was one of those standard green, 2-burner Coleman numbers, and getting it going was a fussy process that involved pressurizing the white gas tank and then lighting it with a match.

Finally, Barry had a burner going, and Kris set his pan of fish on the stove and resumed cooking.

BANG! The stove gave off a small explosion, and Kris leaped, hitting his head on the cabin top and swearing again.

"What was that?" he exclaimed.

Barry had jumped up and was already relighting the stove. "Nothing, just a little problem we've been having with the valve lately," he said.

As the one who did most of the cooking, I had been living with this "little" problem for a couple of weeks. I was terrified of loud explosions, and I hated the way Barry downplayed it. "It's nothing, just a little steam," he'd say, elbowing me out of the way and relighting it. I was secretly glad to see that I wasn't the only one disturbed by our stove's misbehavior.

BANG! The second time the stove exploded and went out, Kris didn't jump quite as high, but he did ask, suspiciously, "What kind of fuel does this thing use, anyway?"

"Just regular Coleman fuel," said Barry. Kris pressed him for more details, and when he admitted it was white gas, Kris put his foot down.

"Get that thing off the boat!" he said to Barry, pulling out a small electric toaster. I couldn't help but giggle as he forced the irregular pieces of fish into the slots. They tasted fine, but for the rest of that appliance's life, the toast would always be a little fishy.

A few days later, Barry and I had gone to sleep in the Squid Wagon in our campground when someone tapped on the window. I sat up and started shrieking. I had learned from experience that screaming was the thing to do in such situations.

"What? What?" said Barry, groping around for his glasses.

Only a few weeks earlier, in Newfoundland, we'd been sleeping in the back of the Squid Wagon when someone tried the passenger door to see if it was locked. That time, I had stayed quiet, so the thief went around and broke the driver's side window! Once he did that, I screamed loudly for so long that he was probably ten miles away by the time the police arrived. If I had screamed sooner, we might not have had to replace the driver's window.

This time, I looked out and saw that it was Kris in the moonlight, wondering why I was screaming at the top of my lungs. He held up something large and rectangular for me to see, and I stopped screaming and opened the door.

"Look what I found for you!" he said, holding up a two-burner propane Coleman stove. He continued, "I was on the way back from the pub, and people are putting their trash out for tomorrow. This was sitting on the curb. All you need is a propane bottle to see if it works."

That trash pile stove still works perfectly, eight years later.

When we finally said farewell to Kris in Lunenburg, I put him our address book. We wrote emails and shared our news on blogs. Then we got Skype, and Facebook, so we could keep up with both the mundane happenings and the exciting developments in each others' lives.

A few months after we met, he returned to South Africa to check his rental property and apply for an extended Canadian visa. He had

Kris

a dream to buy a small steel boat and sail the Northwest Passage, to finish his circumnavigation of North and South America.

It was in South Africa that he had the most exciting, unexpected development.

When his Canadian visa came in, he celebrated by inviting a new lady friend out to dinner. But falling in love changed his plans completely, so that he never needed that visa. Instead of a grueling solo trip through the Northwest Passage, Kris got married and sailed with his wife and son in the Bahamas and the Mediterranean.

Over the years, Barry and I have gotten together with Kris for so many zany adventures that even half a world away, we share a plethora of inside jokes. My favorites are the ones about meeting your best friend in a laundromat.

I will be forever grateful that my cruising notebook wasn't hidden under a piece of dirty laundry when Kris walked by. It was the notebook that caught his eye and told him we were kindred spirits.

Luckily, some kindred spirits are much easier to spot. One of my absolute favorites is Libby, who literally has a giant sign over her head that announces "Kindred Spirit."

It was in the middle of winter, in coastal North Carolina, and I was completely miserable. Barry and I were living aboard *Flutterby* in a boatyard, doing a refit. The boat was a wreck, with tools and parts everywhere, barely enough room to sit down, and a tiny heater that only raised the temperature to 40 degrees Fahrenheit.

On the coldest day, when I couldn't take any more, I fled. I didn't have anyplace to go, but I drove for miles on lonely backroads with the heater in the car going full-blast.

On a previous driving expedition, I had noticed a tearoom sitting on a desolate road, on the way from "nowhere" to "the end of the known world." I headed that way, my heart set on a pot of tea and a warm blueberry scone.

Even as I drove, I started to fret. A voice in my head asked, What if the place was closed? After all, it was midweek and off-season. To drive over 20 miles, to waste time and gas, was probably a fool's errand.

I gave the voice in my head a stern talking-to. I told myself that if I couldn't have tea and a scone, I'd keep going, to a cafe up the road, for a cup of coffee and a piece of pie.

But what if the cafe was closed, too? said the voice in my head.

Then I'd stop at the gas station and treat myself to a Coke and a package of Ho-Hos.

When I arrived at the tearoom, there were colorful flags flapping and a car in front. The Kindred Spirit was open for business.

Inside, I found a gift shop full of elegant teapots and cozies, pillows, handbags, and jewelry. The owner encouraged me to choose any tea from a large display of flavors with evocative names like "Eye of the Tiger" and "Cupid's Bling." She took me into a large room with Victorian decor and seated me in a wing chair in front of a table with a lace tablecloth. Before she went to brew my pot of Lemon Souffle Rooibos, she put soothing ballads on the stereo.

In my dispirited state, I felt like such a welcomed, honored guest that it brought tears to my eyes. I wished I could spend more time in this cozy, civilized place.

My wish came true.

When we started talking, I discovered a true kindred spirit in Libby. I offered to help her with some projects, which gave me an excuse to spend a day in the tearoom every week. That was my favorite day of the week, the day when the two of us could hang out and drink tea and talk about everything (and everybody!) under the sun.

Being with Libby was like spending time with an artist, because like a painter, she interpreted the world for me in a colorful, original way. She had an incredible knowledge of wildlife and could identify the dozens of birds who came to her feeders. When an albino mockingbird took up residence in her neighborhood, she brought photographs to show me. She kept in touch with local ornithologists, and told me where I could go to see sandhill cranes behind the old elementary school. She fed foxes and stray cats, and in addition to two cats at home, she had a rescue cat named Maggie May living at the shop.

When I first found the tearoom, my impression of Libby was a polite, reserved Southern hostess, the kind of person who says "Bless your heart," and means it. Behind the scenes, though, she was one of the funniest people I have ever known. She knew everyone in the area and could do a wicked impression of the ones she didn't like, as well as some of the ones she did.

Libby

She showed me how to be a steel magnolia, to laugh in the face of adversity. She taught me to say "Bless your heart" with a straight face and mean the exact opposite.

In the course of the next year, I am certain that Libby and I drank enough tea to float a 33-foot sailboat. I can't think of any other reason why Barry and I would finally launch *Flutterby* after three years in the boatyard where she had literally put down roots (we had blackberry vines growing up around the hull). I didn't need to make an entry for Libby in my address book. I had her number memorized, and I could drive to "Hooterville" (which is where she jokingly said the tearoom was located) with my eyes closed.

Despite the sunny, tropical adventures we had planned, it broke my heart to sail south and leave my best friend behind. I consoled myself with a line from Anne of Green Gables: "True friends are always together in spirit."

Because of people like Libby and Kris, I keep breaking the rules, the ones about not taking candy from strangers. Over and over, people I have never met before have walked straight into my heart, often by way of my funny bone.

I never know when a chance meeting will profoundly change my life. Perhaps a chance meeting with *me* will change someone else's life. That's a profound thought.

Every day, in every moment, I am always looking for the next stranger with candy. They might be anywhere, not just in a laundromat.

Once I find them, we will never be strangers again.

DON'T BE A STRANGER

> "What do you want to do today?" I asked Philip.
>
> "Let's go out and find some strangers to talk to!" he said. And we did.

Philip's enthusiasm is proof that we can all do this, if we want to. He *swore* he was a terminally shy guy for the first 55 years of his life.

Each of us, in our own way, can learn to connect with strangers and people whose lives are different from our own. We can reach out to them without judgment, and we can let them reach out to us.

It's not exactly clear who's giving the candy and who's getting it. When we make a real human connection, when we listen to someone's story, we both win.

If you would like to learn more about how to get candy from strangers and share your stories about the amazing people you meet, please visit my webpage: **1meps.com/candy**

I look forward to hearing from you!

meps